'This is vintage Bryn. His insights into discipling, his perception regarding coaching and his wisdom concerning mentoring shine throughout this book.'

Geoff Feasey, author and member of Elim Pentecostal Church's National Leadership Team

'Bryn's analytical insights plus emotional awareness provide true wisdom from a real all-rounder.'

David Taylor, Pastor, Bushey Baptist Church

'It is the most comprehensive single guide to the subject I have come across as a pastor – widely accessible with practical applications. Another must-have tool for leadership development in the local church.'

Jonathan Le Tocq, The King's Church, Guernsey

By the same author:
Leadership Tool Kit (Kingsway Publications, 2002)
Small Group Know How (Monarch Books, 2001)

Discipling, Coaching, Mentoring

BRYN HUGHES

KINGSWAY PUBLICATIONS
EASTBOURNE

ISBN 1 84291 052 3

Published by
KINGSWAY COMMUNICATIONS LTD
Lottbridge Drove, Eastbourne BN23 6NT, England.
Email: books@kingsway.co.uk

Book design and production for the publishers by
Bookprint Creative Services, P.O. Box 827, BN21 3YJ, England.
Printed in Great Britain.

Dedication

To my brother, Gareth:
a faithful, diligent friend who models true
servanthood better than anyone else I know.

And to Dave Cormack, again!
Thank you for illustrating so much of the message of this book
towards me, by coaching, mentoring and true friendship.
Much of the best fruit from my work nowadays is
because you believed in me.

Acknowledgements

To Dr David Cormack, Tim Goss, Tony Horsfall and Alan Preston. Many thanks for your comments on the draft text. The end product has been vastly improved by your care, insights and feedback.

Also thanks to Tony again, and to Jonathan Dunning, for their contributions to the chapter on journalling.

Robert McLeish – thanks for your research into the questions of Jesus and for sharing many seminars and travels together.

Thank you, Dr Steve Brady, for writing the Foreword.

Lastly, thanks to my wife, Vicky, for lots of detailed work on the text and for your sacrifices during the two years when this book was being written.

Contents

Foreword

I have had the happy privilege, over some thirty years in full-time Christian service, of participating in and leading team ministries. I am sorry I did not have a book like this when I set out. Now I know what I have been doing wrong all these years! Like me, I believe you are going to enjoy this book, and here's why.

First, you will find yourself in the hands of an experienced and wise guide who continues to practise what he preaches in these pages. I know what an enormous help he has been to Moorlands College for our own development in various key areas. Moreover, I deeply value his personal friendship and encouragement.

Second, you will find his style immediately accessible and engaging. Again and again in reading these pages, I have thought, 'Ah, now I see it, now I see why.' Bryn takes us step by step through the often confused roles of mentor and coach and how that intersects with biblical discipling.

Third, this is not merely a 'how to' book. You will discover that you are being personally cross-examined in the process of learning how to function better in your role of discipler/ disciple. There are questions to answer – and thankfully a chapter on how to ask them! – and visual diagrams to help you think through issues. Moreover, the dark side of our human nature is not ignored!

Fourth, you will pick up some very helpful quotes, illustrations and 'one liners', for instance: 'Programmes are really an attempt to do discipling on the cheap'; 'Discipling is costly'; 'Messy services are necessary' (consult Chapter 14 for context for that one); 'In the rough and tumble of discipling, we will need buckets of sacrificial love to sustain us.'

Fifth, Bryn reminds us that discipleship needs to be relational and purposeful. I know some of my friends wince at the prospect of intentional discipleship, saying, 'Leave them to God; let go and let God do it.' Well, that is also intentional discipleship: i.e. their intention is to do little or nothing! So he reminds us of the biblical mandates we have from the Lord Jesus and his apostles 'to make disciples'. From where I sit, and from my travels around the UK and beyond, it is a task that the church needs to take far more seriously and urgently than she has been doing for some decades now.

Finally, if you are involved in any form of team ministry – and if not, why not? – this book is a must. It will challenge, inform and inspire you. At least, that has been my experience. Enjoy!

Dr Steve Brady
Principal, Moorlands College

Introduction

In my early days as a Christian, there were two areas of the spiritual life that were renowned as difficult: evangelism and discipleship. These were the real mountains to climb. These were the challenges that reputedly few individuals or churches could master. It was a pity, really, because between them they cover so much of the Christian life. Christians who do not share their faith effectively with others or grow closer to God have precious little to offer or look forward to in their Christian walk on this earth.

Over the second half of the twentieth century, landmark ministries emerged that broke down the barriers of evangelism. In my limited view of the post-war world, Billy Graham was the champion. He gave mass evangelism an acceptable and modern face. Nearer the end of the century, there was a much greater emphasis and a shift to our personal responsibility for evangelism, highlighted by various initiatives, including *Evangelism Explosion* and the Decade of Evangelism.

Now we have Alpha. The advent and development of the Alpha courses has had a significant impact, not only across

11

the UK, but in many other countries. The wide participation is not just geographical, for the materials are accepted and welcomed right across the whole spectrum of churches. Not only have many people become Christians, but Alpha has made evangelism a user-friendly activity, at least in part. The fear factor has diminished. Far more people have shared their faith and (surprise, surprise) they have lived to tell the tale! Certainly we have no grounds for complacency, but evangelism recently has become more 'manageable' to the ordinary Christian. But the other mountain still beckons.

I have the privilege of working with many church leaders and visiting many churches. There is one God and he speaks with only one voice, so when a wide variety of leaders from many different traditions seem to be hearing similar things, I get excited and take notice. Their focus has turned to discipleship. In the last few years, this has been the main issue that leaders are addressing, with varying degrees of success. 'How can I disciple my flock?' is the frequent cry. Some leaders and ministers seem paralysed, conscious of the great commission to 'make disciples', yet awed by the challenge of making discipleship a way of life in their churches. Other churches and leaders have made some initial progress by focusing on a segment of the church membership, often the youth group or new converts. Now they are considering how to produce widespread adoption of discipleship across the whole membership.

Other churches have developed courses on discipleship, but have come to recognise the limitations of their materials. The products were helpful for perhaps a six-month duration, but there is a growing recognition that discipleship should be a lifetime mentality for all Christians.

Those are the concerns of leaders. Members are simultaneously expressing their concerns about the same problem, but naturally from a different angle. Folk who have been Christians for perhaps five years and reached an understanding of the core drills of the spiritual army are asking about further and continuous growth and development. Questions about the practicalities of discipleship are common. People are recognising that you can profess to be a Christian without living as a disciple; it's a frustrating experience in many ways, and the expectations of some believers have now grown higher than this mediocrity.

Thankfully, there is a very important and satisfying link between evangelism and discipleship. The twin mountains of yesteryear are far from mutually exclusive. For those who are concerned that an emphasis on discipleship will produce introverted churches yet again, fear not! A key fruit of effective discipleship must be an increase in evangelistic passion. As we grow closer to God, we will want to tell other people about the importance of that relationship to us. I am saddened, by contrast, in some churches that I know well, where the ministry of the pastor/teacher has not produced the right fruit. Long sermons and deep 'meaningful' times of worship (also long!) have not produced a real increase in spirituality. Discipleship, including teaching, that does not produce passionate evangelism deserves serious scrutiny, because it is failing in one of its purposes.

The principal activities in discipleship revolve around the personal relationship between the individual disciple and Jesus. That may not be apparent or fairly represented by the pages of this book. I don't feel qualified to write about the devotional life, as I don't regard my own times with God as exemplary to others. But the other activity, 'making disciples', involves interaction with other people, and that is the area I want to focus on in this book. I will use the term 'discipleship' to mean 'being a disciple' and 'discipling' to cover 'making disciples and developing people'. Additionally, I will retain discipleship for the few occasions when I am referring to the combined package. Discipling is the lesser part of the combination and, however well done, can never be a substitute for meeting with God personally and being immersed in his word.

One delegate at a seminar recently took exception to my use of the verb 'discipling', noting that biblically there is only a noun form. While technically I accepted the correction, the concept of our involvement in the activity of making disciples and the dynamic nature of language gives me all I need to be comfortable with 'discipling' as a verb. It's very proactive.

I want to make a contribution to the 'how' of discipling, because so many disciples and leaders are asking about this. If I am qualified to write in this way, then it is because I am a technician, a practitioner. The germ of the idea for this book came in about 1993; I immediately felt a strong sense that I should gain further experience first, then teach around the subjects of my title before finally writing about them.

An introduction to a book is not the place to stray into too much detail; the individual chapters are designed to explore the practicalities and are fairly self-contained. However, there is one tension that we should label right from the beginning: discipling is both *relational* and *purposeful*. The potential to create an imbalance and favour one end of this axis disproportionately cannot be avoided. Even yesterday I experienced it afresh. My wife and I have been asked to have some sustained input into a family in our own church. Fortunately, it is acknowledged by all parties that there are some serious issues to address. We start with a good track record of friendship between the families. Yet looking forward, I can see possible tensions. Will the relationship be as good in two years' time? How quickly can we make progress? How do we maintain a balance of relationship and purposeful discipling? The situation feels challenging but essentially is no different from scenarios that you may be facing, based on compassion for people *and* a desire for true discipling. In practice, this tension proves largely theoretical, but in prospect it seems very daunting.

There is another aspect to my experience that I will be able to draw on. I was privileged as a new Christian in the 1960s to be part of an excellent church youth group. When I have talked about this book recently with the leadership from those days, they have been a little embarrassed and reckon that most of their good practice was subconscious. Nevertheless, they helped build good foundations into my Christian life. Similarly, my first years in teaching were in an outstanding school where I had a housemaster and a head of department who were wise people and prepared to pour the benefits of their experiences into me. They were also good friends and there was no tension of roles. A couple of other senior staff were just as significant, but without formal positions of line management.

The principles I gleaned from these two seasons in my life, one in the church and one at work, were virtually identical. There was one common ingredient in all the people who made those significant positive contributions. It wasn't what they said that drew my attention initially; it was what they were doing. Their advice came out of practice and experience, and they had impressive track records. There was no attempt to drown me in theory. But I've known the arid times as well, sometimes for prolonged periods. Indeed, they have contributed to this book. Bad experiences can also contribute to learning, partly by offering such a contrast.

As you start reading, I trust that you will continue to enjoy your voyage of discovery, including finding out more about yourself. There really are no shortcuts. In the last week, I've had four phone calls asking me for my recommendations for questionnaires that help people identify their gifts. Certainly some products are better than others, and are part of better processes, but are we in danger of missing the point? Caricaturing more than slightly, it seems that Jesus, Peter, Paul and Barnabas, for example, managed to do discipling very well without such aids. Are we really looking for a twenty-minute tick-box questionnaire that will reveal the richness of our gifts? Thank God that the tapestry is not that simple nor so easily understood. The process of discovery is a lifetime privilege.

The essence of this book is summarised in the title. The words 'coaching' and 'mentoring' are culled from the secular world, but are still based on the desire to see people develop. By using a distinction between them wisely, we can gain some insights into how discipling can be done well. Much of what we may initially presume to be secular understanding is actually firmly rooted in Scripture – it's our inheritance.

1

The Hallmarks of Jesus' Discipling

The life of Jesus on this earth was in distinct phases. For about thirty years he lived a very 'normal' life, being part of a family, being gainfully employed and suffering many of the temptations that we face. The main incidents recorded in some detail which mark him out distinctively are his miraculous birth and his authoritative contributions in the Temple at a very tender age (Luke 2:41–48). The next three years were his overt ministry, culminating in his death and resurrection.

I have sometimes wondered why he didn't go to the cross sooner. The answer presumably is that he had to fulfil all prophecy. What was the additional impact and fruit of those three years? He left us with a great legacy of teaching and he showed us how to train disciples. As an introduction to seminars on this subject, I frequently ask groups, 'What were the hallmarks of Jesus' training of the disciples?' and log the answers on a flipchart. Groups have invariably produced lists similar to the bulk of the headings we shall discuss in this chapter.

17

The blueprint

The blueprint for good discipleship is obviously well known in a theoretical sense, but not so frequently applied. The next few pages will serve as a reference for much of the rest of the book. The key characteristics of his training (in no particular order of priority) were as follows:

- He loved them.
- He taught them.
- He gave them tasks to do and commissioned them.
- He gave them authority as well as jobs.
- He spent time with them away from the public arena.
- He recognised that they were all different and called them individually.
- He modelled things to them.
- He prayed for them.
- He encouraged them.
- He rebuked them.
- He had legitimate circles of intimacy.

He loved them

Probably this is the basis for all effective discipleship. I sometimes wonder whether Jesus liked all the people he called to work with him. But loving is much deeper than liking; not only is it less vulnerable to fluctuations in our feelings, it is eternal. Love overcame his frustrations, his disappointments and even the fact that one betrayed him. Love is the basis of compassion. Its durability underpins the cost of discipleship.

Peter's denials of Jesus are reported in all the gospels, but only in Luke do we read, 'The Lord turned and looked straight at Peter' (Luke 22:60). Peter must have felt all manner of emotional reactions as he remembered Jesus' prediction. But what did he see in the eyes of Jesus? Pain? Sadness? Disappointment? I suspect it was the love that Jesus communicated that really broke him and reduced him to tears.

The teaching of Jesus is unequivocal: 'As the Father has loved me, so have I loved you' (John 15:9); 'As I have loved you, so you must love one another' (John 13:34). Clearly there will be a limit to the duration of our discipling relationships if we cannot fulfil this principal commandment.

He taught them

Substantial sections of the gospels are devoted to recording the teachings of Jesus, including many chapters in their entirety. Example passages include the Sermon on the Mount (Matthew 5–7), the long discourse (John 14–16), some parables (Matthew 13) and the apocalyptic material (Mark 13). In terms of illustrating the training of disciples, the methods and style of his work will prove just as important to us as the content of his teaching. He used parables, stories that would be relevant to his listeners, although he did not give everybody a full explanation (Matthew 13:18). He also checked to see how much they had understood. After all, if there's been no learning, there's been no teaching! He interspersed his teaching with questions ('Who do you say I am?' and 'Which of these three do you think was a neighbour to the man who fell into the hands of robbers?' Matthew 16:15 and Luke 10:36).

Interestingly, Jesus also experienced the same difficulty that all teachers face today. He taught his disciples about the forthcoming events of holy week three times, as we see in each of the synoptic gospels (Matthew 16–17, 20; Mark 8–10; Luke 9, and twice in 18). They just didn't get it, despite the fact that they had the perfect teacher! Their paradigms about proper messiahs prevented them from understanding. Nevertheless, Jesus not only taught the disciples, but he repeated the messages when necessary. Later they would have the information in their minds for when they most needed it.

He gave them tasks to do and commissioned them

There appear to be three phases within Jesus' development of the disciples. In the early chapters of all the gospels, the focus is very much on Jesus. He selected the team, he did the work, he set the standards, he challenged their understanding and expectations and he taught them. Then progressively, as we move through the three years of ministry, the involvement and participation of the disciples increases. However, the ultimate goal of leadership is not just to produce 'followership', but instead faithful people who will go beyond their leaders to scale even greater heights. Initially the functions asked of the disciples were relatively mundane; the tasks delegated to them were apparently uninspiring. In time, the jobs became increasingly demanding, culminating in the Great Commission.

There is a similar important phase for all leaders who are discipling today. The old throwaway line 'You will know who the leaders are – they've got followers' has some merit; at least the leader is going somewhere! There has to be a middle stage, when the leader is more 'hands off' and there might be more mistakes made too! As with the disciples responding to Jesus, it may well be that today's disciples also make progress by doing simple tasks well. There will be a build-up of trust and evidence of faithfulness that leads to further opportunities.

However, we need to recognise an important difference between Jesus and most other people involved in discipling. He had all the authority within his team to offer opportunities to the other members. Not every discipler is in that position because they do not all lead teams. I've known a significant number of people trying to fulfil the biblical mandate to make disciples, who have to canvas elders and ministers in order to create the situations where their disciples could grow. This is one obvious respect in which not all disciplers can follow Jesus' methods.

Here are just a few examples of opportunities of service given to various groups of disciples:

- Luke 10:1–23   The sending out of the seventy-two – their first significant opportunity.
- Matthew 14:13–21 The feeding of the five thousand.
- Matthew 15:32–37 The feeding of the four thousand.
- Matthew 21:1–3   Collecting the Palm Sunday transport.
- Mark 14:12–16   Volunteering to make the arrangements for the Passover meal.
- Mark 16:15   'Go into all the world and preach the good news to all creation.'

He gave them authority as well as jobs

It's not sufficient just to create opportunities. Research is quite clear about the reasons why delegated tasks can and do go wrong. Perhaps surprisingly, the majority of the causes can be attributed to the delegator, not the delegate. Within the possible reasons, one of the major factors is that the delegator can be unwilling to delegate sufficient authority along with the task, often under the auspices of 'the buck stops here'. Right from the beginning, in the creation account of Genesis chapter 1 (v. 26), God delegated authority when he gave man the rule over all the creatures. Of course, you increase the possibility that people will make mistakes as you give them more authority! Jesus demonstrated the principle in Luke 9:1: 'When Jesus had called the Twelve together, he gave them power and authority to drive out all demons and to cure diseases.' This is not an isolated illustration of Jesus imparting authority. The same feature is evident in some of the examples about tasks in the previous section of this chapter.

He spent time with them away from the public arena

Making disciples is a very labour intensive business. Jesus spent substantial time working primarily with twelve people and, in particular, with an inner group of three within the twelve. It would seem from the Scriptures that they spent virtually all of their time together, not just a couple of evenings per week. Even then, he lost one of the twelve, and one of his closest companions denied him at a very late stage in their time together on this earth.

In training disciples, there is always an agenda, but that doesn't mean that the process has to be intense. Progress is not made by stringing together deep, soul-searching sessions without any interludes. Friendship needs to be built by doing ordinary things together, as well as the more overtly spiritual activities. As the Alpha initiative has shown us, eating together offers both fun and a high degree of intimacy. Some of these principles that are working increasingly well for evangelism can be equally applied to discipleship.

I can recall other mundane activities that have moved some of my friendships forward. One friendship (that had a substantial discipling component) progressed dramatically by going to watch soccer matches together; the time spent travelling was just as important as watching Oxford United play. (Hardly surprising, I hear some of the sporting among you saying!) Heavy manual work can bring an informal team

THE HALLMARKS OF JESUS' DISCIPLING

together; there's nothing like barrowing a few cubic metres of ready-mix concrete to cause people to bond. Nowadays our own church leadership go away together for five days each year; the 'spiritual' sessions are precious but the informal time proves just as beneficial, albeit in a different way.

Here are some of the occasions in the gospels when specific mention is made of Jesus doing ordinary things with his team:

* Mark 2:15   Having dinner at Levi's house.
* John 2:2   The wedding at Cana in Galilee.
* John 3:22   Going out into the Judean countryside and spending time together.
* Luke 9:18   Praying in private with the disciples.
* Mark 2:23   Walking in the cornfields.

Please remember the overview message at the beginning of this section, as well as considering these few specific examples: Jesus invested the bulk of three years in discipling twelve people.

He recognised that they were all different and called them individually

Any discipling relationship requires the agreement of both parties. This is very apparent in the early chapters of the gospels when Jesus invited the disciples to join him. In the NIV, the heading above the relevant section of the three synoptic gospels says 'The calling of the first disciples'. To some extent, this subtitle is in danger of detracting from Jesus' role by turning the focus on to the disciples. He selected them; he called them in very specific ways, because he knew that these were the right men for him to develop over the next three years. They responded immediately and wholeheartedly to establish the partnerships. (For example, Peter's call is in Luke 5:3–11 and Nathanael's call is in John 1:47.)

A big danger in many discipling programmes is that of treating everybody alike. The erroneous assumption is that people need to learn the same things, at the same rate and in the same way. I suppose that if such a programme were truly successful, all the participants would emerge identical! According to the detail we are given in the gospels, and there isn't much about nine of the disciples, the disciples were very different characters and Jesus treated them accordingly. He even varied his leadership style towards Peter during the three years of their time together. Initially he was much more directive, and latterly much more personal. The approach of trying to devise the universal programme is far removed from the biblical model. Discipling is not cloning.

He modelled things to them

Jesus showed his disciples how to do things. Naturally, as he remained perfect during his time on this earth, he was the perfect role model on character issues (see Hebrews 4:15). But additionally he embodied all the gifts, so he was an example to them in every way. He healed the sick using a rich variety of methods. So when he commanded them to go out and heal the sick, he had shown them how to do it. He challenged the social attitudes of the day, not principally by telling people what to think, but by having lunch with tax collectors (Luke 5:29) and by chatting to the Samaritan woman (John 4). He confronted the key religious figures of the day and challenged their attitudes towards the Sabbath (Luke 6) and style of prayer. If you wanted to be a radical, you could watch Jesus, not just listen to him. Rather than writing a book about deliverance ministry, he actually cast out demons.

By doing things perfectly, Jesus generated a natural desire in the disciples to learn and improve. After he had prayed, the disciples asked him to teach them: 'Once when Jesus was praying in private and his disciples were with him...' (Luke 9:18) and 'One day Jesus was praying in a certain place. When he finished, one of his disciples said to him, "Lord, teach us to pray, just as John taught his disciples"' (Luke 11:1). Perhaps above all, his relationship with the Father was the linchpin of his ministry and he showed them how to foster that key relationship.

From this section, we see one of the major differences between Jesus and ourselves when it comes to discipling. He was omni-gifted, so he could model everything perfectly. If you had been one of the twelve, whatever your aspirations in ministry, you could have learnt just by watching Jesus and copying what he did. We too should treat modelling as an important method of discipling, but would do well to remember that we're not called to model all of the gifts! The modelling approach to discipling is valid, effective and good, but incomplete. Any attempt to rely exclusively on this style of discipling smacks of arrogance, for you cannot develop anybody beyond your own competence in a given field by this method. We will look at alternative approaches to discipleship in later chapters.

He prayed for them

Discipling is a spiritual battle and victory therefore depends on fighting with spiritual weapons. Most steps of significant progress in the lives of disciples are not won on the basis of logical argument; it's revelation that wins the day – just as at the point of conversion. There is a life change when knowledge drops from the head to the heart, as opposed to theoretical

understanding and insight. Often, therefore, the key to bringing about major change is prayer, for often we will reach the
point where there is nothing further we can humanly do to help
the disciple forward. Prayer, allied to love, should be the first
and ongoing resort.

I am always a little cautious when people seem to want to
do the bulk of the praying with the disciple. There is the
danger that subconsciously the activity of prayer masks yet
another attempt at persuasion, or that the discipler would like
to be in on the act and take some of the credit. While praying
together obviously has a place, sometimes we have to do some
serious graft in private. Certainly there are specific references
in the gospels to Jesus praying in private, as well as passages
when he prays over his disciples (Luke 22:32; John 17:20–26).

He encouraged them

We don't read many words of personal encouragement from
Jesus to any of the disciples, but I imagine that they carried a
great deal of weight when he did speak them. His words would
not have been shallow, empty, ritualistic or cheaply earned.
Encouragement and rebuke are both forms of feedback and
we shall consider them further in Chapter 9. Examples from
the gospels include:

'Blessed are you, Simon son of Jonah, for this was not revealed to
you by man, but by my Father in heaven. And I tell you that you
are Peter, and on this rock I will build my church, and the gates of
Hades will not overcome it.' (Matthew 16:17–18)

'In this world you will have trouble. But take heart! I have overcome the world.' (John 16:33)

Encouragement is not just praise; it is anything that puts fresh heart into the disciple.

He rebuked them

I have been careful to talk about encouraging before rebuking! Jesus did not refrain from rebuking his disciples for fear that they would run off. Here are some examples: 'You of little faith, why are you so afraid?' (Matthew 8:26); 'O unbelieving generation . . . how long shall I stay with you? How long shall I put up with you?' (the context is the healing of the dumb boy, immediately after the Transfiguration in Mark 9:19); 'When he was in the house, he asked them, 'What were you arguing about on the road?' But they kept quiet . . .' (Mark 9:33).

The original Greek word for rebuke (*elencho*) translates something like 'to convict in such a way that they feel ashamed'. Throughout the gospels, Jesus is highly confrontational. We need to explode the myth of 'gentle Jesus, meek and mild'. With people like Nicodemus and the rich young ruler, he went straight for the jugular. It's not easy, but hopefully we can give and receive within the discipling relationship without taking offence and without jeopardising the fundamental bond.

He had legitimate circles of intimacy

Many leaders today find it difficult to spread their time and efforts unevenly. They feel guilty and think it is 'unfair' to select a few people for the bulk of their discipling. More probably they are afraid of what other people might think! Jesus had no such inhibitions. Certainly there were times when he ministered to large crowds, but more frequently his focus came down to seventy-two, twelve or three people. The weight of evidence in the records of the gospels, especially after the initial call of the twelve, is that he focused substantially on Peter, James and John. This can be seen from the range of his conversations, what was offered to them and what was asked of them.

Conclusion

I've tried to select the qualities of Jesus' ministry that seem to be very important as we are involved in discipling today. Many other characteristics deserve a brief mention. Being without sin, he perfectly illustrated patience and approachability. He listened to his disciples. He saw potential in them and he envisioned them. He was honest with them and he shared his vulnerability. If at any point we are not sure how discipling should work, there is for our reference a record of a three-year ministry that changed the world.

Check your own discipling technique against that of our Lord:

Qualities of Jesus' discipling	Comments on my own discipling
Loving	
Teaching	
Giving tasks	
Giving authority as well as jobs	

Spending time

Treating all individually

Modelling

Praying

Encouraging

Rebuking

Having legitimate circles of intimacy

_____

2

The Nuts and Bolts of Discipling

At the very end of Matthew's Gospel, we have the mandate known as the Great Commission:

> 'Therefore go and make disciples of all nations, baptising them in the name of the Father, and of the Son and of the Holy Spirit, and teaching them to obey everything I have commanded you. And surely I am with you always, to the very end of the age.' (Matthew 28:19–20)

Mark is the only other author to quote this conversation and he is just as unequivocal.

Although Jesus was speaking to the eleven disciples, I think most people assume that this instruction applies to all of us, throughout the centuries. The logic is that *we* are told to preach the good news to all creation – a task that would physically have been beyond the initial eleven disciples. In the Great Commission, there is no mention of converts, only disciples; seeing people come to faith is only the beginning of the journey. My conclusion from these scriptures is that we should all be disciples and that we should all be discipling others.

The *Concise Oxford Dictionary* defines a disciple as a 'follower, adherent, of any leader of thought, art, etc.'. There are therefore disciples of other people or philosophies; the word is not used exclusively about Jesus. In Isaiah (19:11) there is reference to 'a disciple of the ancient kings'. Stanley and Clinton, in their book *Connecting* (p. 48), have produced a useful working definition: 'Discipling is a relational process in which a more experienced follower of Christ shares with a newer believer the commitment, understanding and basic skills necessary to know and obey Jesus Christ as Lord.' I don't think that I would want to limit discipling to these basics, but I fully agree with the pragmatic heart of their statement. The disciples we are hoping to make will be followers of Jesus, the personal Saviour; anything that we undertake must contribute towards their growth and development in that walk. Our aim in discipling is to see people who will acknowledge him as Lord, and increasingly serve him. It must include loving him and praising him just for who he is.

The quality and depth of what we are trying to produce is easily under-estimated. Our ultimate goal is not just growth in those we disciple; we want them to become sufficiently mature and equipped that they can continue the process into succeeding spiritual generations. We need the heart and mind of Paul when we disciple: 'And the things you have heard me say in the presence of many witnesses entrust to reliable men who will also be qualified to teach others' (2 Timothy 2:2). He lists four spiritual generations here:

- me (i.e. Paul)
- you (initially Timothy and now us, his readers)

- reliable men
- others

Believe me, discipling with the intention of reaching the fourth generation is quite different in outlook and practice from merely helping the second generation. I can recall more than one occasion in my earlier blundering attempts at discipleship when it became apparent how little lasting fruit had been produced. Probably I would have been more successful if I had treated people differently, encouraging and expecting them in turn to produce further generations of spiritual growth. Our relationships and processes would of necessity have been somewhat different. This book is dedicated to delivering the highest levels of discipling.

After a basic working definition of the core concept of discipleship, we now need to consider some insights that should help us approach the practice of discipleship. These are my initial practical tips and observations:

1. Growth comes from God, but some comes via other people

All of the potential growth for every disciple comes from God, but some will be channelled through other people. Most of the growth will require the help of other people. We must always remember the interplay between these two dimensions. There are dangers of focusing uniquely on either 'route' to the exclusion of the other. The preference is probably to listen to God and do what he says, and in its purest form there is no better discipleship. But there is the tendency to hear him selectively and to be deaf to areas that are less comfortable. Our hearing is incomplete and imperfect. We can also be tempted to retain our privacy and miss the benefit of doing things together. The other danger is to try to attempt discipling in our own strength with only human help. Discipleship is a spiritual business and we need to use spiritual weapons and tools. It's not difficult for discipling meetings to degenerate into a battle of wills, where the discipler tries to convince the other person about their shortcomings. Conviction is best brought by God, and often the discipler's best contribution is to soak each meeting and its consequences in prayer.

The best judge of when a disciple needs external human help should ideally be the disciple. When they ask for help, they are very likely to act on the advice and outcome; when the initiative is not theirs, the chances of a bad reaction to what is perceived as intrusion are far higher.

2. There are basic and advanced elements of discipleship

It is helpful to liken discipleship to life in the army. To the best of my knowledge, the new recruit starts with some basic drills, including square-bashing and physical fitness. Some of the benefits revolve around teamwork, getting to know each other, and the establishment of discipline within a chain of command. Many of the necessary skills will be practised hundreds of times, so that a soldier can strip and re-assemble his weapon at night or in combat conditions. After the raw recruit has passed through this stage, there is more specialisation. Infantry, artillery, signals and engineering each require a different set of skills. What's more, at this stage you would be trained by specialists in a given technical field.

We can draw a similar contrast in maturity between new converts to faith and mature Christians. The core disciplines of prayer, worship and Bible study must be understood and mastered first. Later on, we will be called to specialise further, according to our gift areas. I've seen quite a few acceptable courses and approaches to training new converts; by far the greater challenge is sustaining discipling with the experienced Christian. The precise scripture 'He trains my hands for battle' interestingly occurs twice (2 Samuel 22:35 and Psalm 18:34) and in a very similar form again in Psalm 144:1. The spiritual application is just as real as the military slant: training and development ought to be ongoing.

3. True discipleship is a process, not a programme

While there are some benefits from basic, written materials as part of a discipling package, there are grave dangers in allowing such a programme to dominate the activities of discipling. As Juan Carlos Ortiz says: 'Discipleship is not a communication of knowledge or information. It is a communication of life. Jesus was concerned with formation, not information' (*Disciple*, p.109). I wholeheartedly concur! Paul sums up the correct approach: 'We loved you so much that we were delighted to share with you not only the gospel of God but our lives as well, because you had become so dear to us' (1 Thessalonians 2:8). This verse illustrates again to us that discipleship must be characterised by the sort of ingredients that we identified in the last chapter from Jesus' approach in the gospels: love, spending vast amounts of time with people, vulnerability, etc.

I want to highlight another danger of creating programmes. Too often the end product to aim for seems to be a 'one size fits-all' tee-shirt. Discipling, especially of mature Christians, must take account of individuality (while not producing independence) partly because we are gifted in different ways and learn in different ways. Programmes have often been strongly favoured because we have not yet produced a culture of discipling in most churches; they offer us a straightforward starting point. But in many cases, programmes are really an attempt to do discipling on the cheap. The process of engaging in life-sharing, as Jesus modelled it, is far more labour intensive than the written approach, but it's the only one that works.

One of my elders did an excellent training evening on discipleship recently. He recalled his teenage years and how, in the initial stages of his Christian walk, some key families had contributed to his development. This is his summary of what they offered him:

- love
- hospitality
- inspiration
- risk-taking
- involvement and participation
- high expectations

None of these contributions is best provided by a programme; they are expressions of life-sharing. I would testify that similar experiences were foundational in my development as well. And at the time we both thought that we were such a blessing to these generous families!

4. We need more than one source of human input in the discipling process

Howard Hendricks, a professor at Dallas Seminary, says:

> As I matured and began to take on more and more protégés, I was careful not to set myself up as the single mentor in anyone's life.

One of the goals is to make a person independently dependent, independent of me and dependent on God and other people that will bring God into their lives. Too much of any one person, no matter how wise that person is, can be a bad thing. It's my judgement that if you give me complete control of any one individual, I will develop a first-class pervert. There would be an exclusivity of input, and the result is that they not only pick up your strengths but they pick up your weaknesses. Furthermore, I don't have everything to give.

I find this practical principle absolutely true and very powerful, even if Howard's imagery is rather unusual! Too often in one-to-one discipling, a possessiveness emerges which hinders the servanthood that needs to undergird the whole process. There is no theoretical reason why this should happen, but experience has told me that the danger is very real. One discipler may still retain oversight of the progress and process, but we all need a range of inputs.

5. Consider what can be achieved in a group and when one-to-one discipling is necessary

There is no reason why some discipling should not be undertaken in a group forum; whenever this is possible, it makes good time management sense to do so. Often a combination of some group work and some further personal time provides an excellent balance and outcome. Teaching can be given to several people simultaneously. The modelling component of discipling and the discussion of the application of the teaching are often best done with individuals; exploration of vision and gift must be done on a one-to-one basis.

6. Most mature Christians can only make significant progress on two or three issues per year

When Juan Carlos Ortiz talks about discipleship in his church, a major breakthrough came when they focused on a limited range of sermon topics per year. The real challenge to all of us is not hearing words, but putting them into practice. I go to many churches where there are fifty-two sermons per year and fifty-two small groups considering the application, a new subject every week. Real growth does not take place at this rate. Mature Christians, who have been round the spiritual block, will not make significant progress on many issues in the course of a year. What were the major growth points for you in the last calendar year? I've found that only a minority of disciples come up with a meaningful answer; seldom will people list five or more areas of growth.

I used to provide consultation to one church in London where the ministry was excellent but the diet was very similar from week to week. Many aspects of the Christian life never got an airing and most areas were glossed over too quickly. I asked them to select one topic and focus on it until there was clear fruit evidenced. They chose the subject of serving. After one month, they telephoned me to say that there was little visible evidence of change within the church. I encouraged them to persevere, with different speakers approaching the theme in a variety of ways. Two months later, the church was transformed. People were volunteering to help the leaders, clean the church building, tidy up the acetates and serve each other.

7. Leaders must model discipling and being discipled

Everything in this book is applicable to all Christians. This is not primarily a book about leadership, but leaders should want to be discipled as much as anybody else. The fact is that they need to be discipled more than other people, for others will copy what they do more than obey what they say. If leaders do not illustrate that discipling matters to them, there can be no real expectation of ordinary members buying into the process.

Leaders will need to work on the same core drills and disciplines as everybody else; walking with God obviously requires relationship with him. The different functions unique to leadership mean that careful thought should be given to their additional development in the leadership areas. Can you make a leader? Some secular authors say that you can because, as they see it, leadership is a set of competencies that can be developed. I think that I would say on balance that you can't. However, I would also try not to over-emphasise the 'anointed' nature of leaders too much; the gift of leadership is only mentioned once (Romans 12:8). Most people in leadership positions, especially if we include all those with any sort of responsibility, can drastically improve their effectiveness by following the discipling principles that are outlined in this book. That includes working at some of the competencies of leadership.

8. Discipleship is often hindered by organisational difficulties

Having excited people about the biblical principles of discipling, I am often asked how we should start developing discipling within a given congregation. That's a relatively easy question: a few people need to commit themselves to being discipled, and then to be available to disciple other folk. Relationship is critical in discipling and structure doesn't initially need to enter the equation when there are only a few one-to-one situations. As soon as we try to widen discipling across a particular church from the few to the many participants, any imposed structure can stifle rapport. Remember our aim: everybody should be discipled, everybody should be discipling, but not all should be discipling all!

We recently faced a similar issue within my own church. A youngster was committed to two gap years after university to take part in an external leadership training programme. As part of the course, each member had a mentor. One of our elders from within the church was mentoring this young man. Their meetings quickly became stilted, functional and dull. Now that the student has been transferred to another mentor, the relationship and learning from the first elder is flowing naturally again. This particular developmental combination of people seems to work better without a structured tag. Too often the early spontaneous initiatives are superseded by lists of pairs of names, without any guarantee that the relationships will spark. We will return to these organisational issues later.

9. A powerful illustration

Stephen Covey, in his book *First Things First*, tells a story that seems to encapsulate some of the best principles of people development (pp. 251–3).

I remember my first experience working with a truly empowering leader. Up to that point in my life, my experience with leadership

was basically with a 'kind control' approach – sort of a benevo-
lent autocracy. Then I came into a situation where I had a new
boss. He didn't see the world through that paradigm at all. He saw
the world through an empowerment paradigm. And my first experience with him utterly disarmed me. I had been put in charge of
a large operation and had many managers reporting to me. My
first contact with this man was one day when he called me on the
phone. As I look back now, I see that all the elements of win-win
– the desired results, guidelines, resources, accountability, and
consequences – were in place through the organization, though
they weren't written down or labelled in that way at the time.

This man said, 'Stephen, I see my role as one of being a source
of help to you, so I would like you to think of me in this way and
let me know what I can do to help you.' I thought to myself, 'Well
that's one of the nicest, most considerate approaches I've ever
heard, but basically he's just trying to build the relationship so he
can come in and make sure things are going right and correct
whatever's wrong.' We judge others by ourselves, and that was the
way I thought. So when I heard his words, I projected my own
motive on his behaviour, unaware of the paradigm out of which
he was operating. He said to me, 'I really mean it, Stephen. I'd like
to come and visit with you, but perhaps this is not an appropriate
time. You may have a number of things going on there, and now
wouldn't be the best time to try to give you help.' And I thought,
'I think he does mean it. It looks like I can call the shots here. He's
not just a hovering supervisor checking up on me. He really wants
to be a source of help.'

Then he said, 'Maybe I could tell you a little about myself and
what my experience has been, and that might give you an idea of
how I could be a resource to you.' Well, he had had something like
twenty-five years more experience than I had. He had a rich
resource base and was extremely wise. But I did have a lot of
things going on at the time, so I said to him, 'Perhaps another time

would be better.' So we put it off. When I did ask him to visit a few weeks later, he took the same attitude. I met him at the airport and asked what he wanted to look into. But he said, 'I'm here to help. We'll do whatever you would like.' So I took him to a meeting, and I said, 'It would help if you were to reinforce this point that I'm trying to get across.' So he did it. Then I made another request and he fulfilled it. Each time he would turn to me and say, 'Is there anything else?' Well, I started feeling, 'I'm the one that's responsible. He's here to help me.' And I started being very open with him. As I would leave a meeting after handling some problems in the way I'd traditionally handled them, I would turn to him and say, 'What do you think about the way I handled that? Was it congruent with your experience?'

And he would answer, 'Well, Stephen, you might consider what they're doing in another division. Or you might consider this other option.' He didn't tell me to do one thing. He basically affirmed my responsibility and my power to make the decisions, but he gave illustrations of examples of things I might consider.

So what happened was that my conscience, not this man, became a dominant force. He had other areas of responsibility. He would leave me and go on to do other things, but my conscience never would. It was always with me. Boy, did I feel responsible! So I started to plumb him for his wisdom and his experience, and he came forth in abundance. But he never told me what to do. He always said, 'You might consider this option' or 'Had you thought about this possibility?' Well, that enthroned my conscience in a way that I had never experienced before.

(The above quotation is used with the permission of the publishers, Simon & Schuster, copyright © Stephen R. Covey, A. Roger Merrill and Rebecca R. Merrill, 1994.)

This story illustrates a very hands-off style of development, which has a very definite place within discipleship. I believe that a valid distinction can be made between coaching and mentoring, and that they offer two distinct arrows in our quiver called discipleship. Both words have a context outside discipleship, represented by the extreme left and right areas on the diagram below. Different authors make different distinctions; unfortunately the two main views are diametrically opposite in their use of the key words. Everyday usage, and the pragmatic benefits that I have observed and experienced, shape the definitions that I will put forward in the next two chapters.

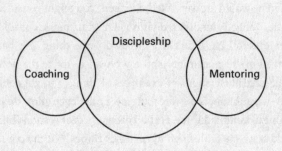

3
Coaching

Coaching and mentoring have sadly become almost synony-mous in common use. The word 'mentoring' is being used with increasing frequency, partly, I suspect, because it seems to have a greater kudos about it. I will split the application of the two words, because they can then point us to two approaches to discipling. We will look at coaching in this chapter and mentoring in the next.

Many of us will have initially met one of these words, coach, in our schooldays in connection with sport. I want to start with that association. Most sports coaches have played to a high standard themselves. In Japan in table tennis, at one time there was a regulation that stipulated that you could not coach to a higher standard than you had played. I have passed my qualification as a football coach. There are two levels called the 'preliminary award' and the 'full badge'. Both are demanding examinations, with a national pass mark below 25 per cent. The biggest difference between the two qualifications is that at the upper level the requirements demand a much better technique in demonstration. The majority of people holding the higher award played professional football and are now employed by the professional clubs. I am fascinated by the rare outstanding manager who has not been an exceptional player, but that would be an unwarranted digression. In the tennis world of today, at long last we have two excellent British players, Tim Henman and Greg Rusedski. Perversely, we haven't got a British coach who can take them to the heights in Grand Slam tournaments because no living British male has reached that standard. I think the general principle is clear: good coaches can develop other people by demonstrating a high level of proficiency in their given area of expertise.

There are some other useful messages that come out of the sporting analogy. People are denied a major route to improvement if they have no role model to emulate. The very top players in any sport have to be incredibly single-minded, possessing a fanatical determination to win, and have to be pioneers and self-starters by nature. The rest of us are privileged to watch and learn from them. At school I was a member of a very strong chess team. One player became an international and has written several books on opening theory, while six other members of that team represented the county and played in the British championships. We were not unique; at one time Dulwich College had most of the best players in Britain (of any age!) in their sixth form. The secret was very simple: youngsters of eleven and twelve played against the top eighteen-year-olds every day. We were bound to improve, and we had been taught to offer the same opportunities in later years to the next school generation. The top schools went decades without producing a weak team.

There is an old adage that practice makes perfect, but there is an underlying assumption that the many repetitions must be based on a sound technique. My experience of cricket is that my batting technique was very moderate, and now that my eyes have deteriorated, the flaws in my technique are painfully exposed. There is a textbook way of doing most things, whether the subject is sport, chess, chemistry, playing a musical instrument, DIY or prayer! The best methods potentially raise the attainment to the maximum; inferior methods will be exposed under extreme pressure.

Eric Parsloe, in his book *Coaching, Mentoring and Assessing* (p.1), comes up with this straightforward definition of coaching: 'A structured two-way process in which individuals develop skills and achieve defined competencies through assessment, guided practical experience and regular feedback.' It is therefore the responsibility and role of the coach to:

- observe
- identify the problem
- demonstrate good practice
- propose solutions
- monitor remedial action

The basic premiss is that the coach knows best! The process of coaching is based on the competence of the coach, skill demonstration and acquisition.

I've discovered that the stage that is missed out most often is the initial phase of observation. Ideally a coach should see someone perform before attempting to help them improve; start with where they are, not with where they ought to be or at some other presumed standard. This danger can be combined with the possibility of under-estimating where they are, and therefore talking down to the disciple. The result will be a weaker relationship, with the likelihood that real progress is hampered.

For the time being, I'm not emphasising the difference between a skill and a gift. I would basically see a gift as coming from God; it cannot be given away. Pragmatically, some gifts seem to be for a short duration, to meet a particular, specific need, but the majority of gifts seem to be more permanently granted ('for God's gifts and his call are irrevocable' – Romans 11:29). A skill is something that can be worked at or mastered by practice. The similarity between gifts and skills is eventually a high degree of proficiency, which can at least in measure be passed on to others. I am not saying that a pupil can acquire the same degree of competence and authority in a particular realm as a gifted person. But the principle that gifts are not only functional, but are also partly used to develop other people, is underlined in Ephesians 4:12: they are 'to prepare God's people for works of service'. There are therefore at least some similarities between gifts and skills, as well as the differences, but I'd rather have an ungifted disciple who is keen to learn the skill than a gifted disciple who is unwilling to learn.

For many people, defining and identifying their gifts proves a difficult and lifelong exercise, as I mentioned in the Introduction. Yet the discovery can and should be fun! Sometimes I think that the problem is partly terminology; just get on and do it without worrying about labelling it! Gerald Coates has said that if you enjoy doing something very much, that's a good indication of it being a gift. In some cases, people don't *feel* gifted! It's not always easy, but we are called to put the authority of Scripture above our feelings. In 1 Corinthians 12–14, there is a block of teaching about spiritual gifts, including: 'to each one the manifestation of the Spirit is given for the common good' (12:7). We are all gifted! Unfortunately, too, leaders sometimes act as though they have a monopoly of the gifts, and by dint of practice they reach a level of competence that denies other people a reasonable opportunity. Sometimes members are reluctant to express their gifts. J. Heinrich Arnold, in his book *Discipleship* (p.116), says in a dialogue with a disciple:

> You write that you are not very gifted. That does not matter. No one has so few gifts that he cannot be moved by God. What matters is that you use the gifts you *do* possess, that they are brought into movement by God. It is never a lack of gifts that is the problem, but a lack of readiness to be used by God.

We must avoid a superspiritual understanding of gifts. We are told to 'eagerly desire the greater gifts' (1 Corinthians 12:31), so there is clearly a differentiation among the gifts. Yet things like counselling and worship leading don't appear in any of the biblical lists. Even more apparently mundane are examples of gifts like financial and numerical dexterity. A good treasurer is a real gift and brings great assurance to many churches. If such accountants recognise that their highly developed gifts come from God, should we treat their contribution as any less significant? In Mission Aviation Fellowship (where I have been on the board), we have some gifted pilots and mechanics; to God be the glory, for some of them are more than just competent!

The diagram below illustrates the stages that the learner goes through in the coaching process. The process of learning to drive a car would illustrate the stages well. Initially the learner may not be doing something very well, and simply doesn't recognise that reality. That's *unconscious incompetence*.

The next step may be triggered by comparison with somebody else, some feedback, or just the feeling that things aren't quite as they should be. 'There's a bit more to this than I realised' is often the comment as the penny drops. Now it's known and recognised that the skill level is low. We've progressed from unconscious to *conscious incompetence*.

The next level is gained by hard slog. We learn routines, do things by rote, and follow checklists. Every step requires thinking about and labelling. Lots of practice leads to *conscious competence*. The final stage, *unconscious competence*, comes when we are sufficiently skilled to do things without thinking.

THE STAGES OF COACHING

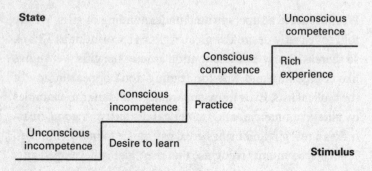

Some practical illustrations

Over the years, as I have worked with missions in Kenya, Vicky and I usually try to visit Nairobi Game Park. Our driver and guide is a missionary with years of experience in the bush and these trips with him have always proved memorable. On one occasion, we saw a lioness with her cubs making a kill. The poor victim was a warthog. Emotionally, we had very mixed feelings; it was brutal and the wretched animal was not dead when the youngsters started tucking in. Yet at the same time, the mother's care of the cubs was very moving. Initially, most of us did not see the little cats; they were kept in the undergrowth by their mum. We had turned off the car engine and were watching through binoculars, but as soon as the engine restarted, the warthog made a bolt for it. The lioness anticipated the event and leapt into action, with the cubs following. At every stage they were shadowing and mimicking their mother's actions. It was a classic coaching scene.

There is a story that was related to me about the yoking of oxen. An old farmer was ploughing with a team of oxen. A visitor was amazed, for one was a huge ox and the other animal was a very small bullock. The ox towered over the little bullock that was sharing the yoke with him. The visitor was perplexed to see two such unequal animals in the yoke together and asked the farmer to explain. It transpired that the little bullock was doing virtually no work, but was being broken into the yoke. This reminded me of Jesus' promise: 'Take my yoke upon you and learn from me, for I am gentle and humble in heart, and you will find rest for your souls. For my yoke is easy and my burden is light' (Matthew 11:29–30).

A close friend of mine is a doctor and he got excited about these two illustrations from the animal kingdom. He said that the training of surgeons follows a similar pattern:

- watch
- do as I say
- see that it works
- practise
- teach others

The patient with the surgeon and the lion cubs' need for food are both life-and-death issues (although the surgeon would hopefully note that trial and error should not be such a prominent part of their recommended learning process!).

Imitators

Much is often made of Paul's injunction that we should be imitators of him. It occurs several times in the New Testament, including:

- 'Therefore I urge you to imitate me' (1 Corinthians 4:16).
- 'We do not want you to become lazy, but to imitate those who through faith and patience inherit what has been promised' (Hebrews 6:12).
- 'Remember your leaders, who spoke the word of God to you. Consider the outcome of their way of life and imitate their faith' (Hebrews 13:7).
- 'Dear friend, do not imitate what is evil but what is good' (3 John 11).

The two Hebrews references are primarily about imitating faith and John uses the word with a warning as well as an encouragement. The context of the Corinthians verse is about being fathers in the gospel. I sense from these passages that imitating good things is a principle worthy of adoption and that there are very real dangers that we can copy bad things unwittingly but just as easily. We should all recognise the responsibility that if anybody looks up to us, then they are in danger of catching some bad features, as well as imitating the good characteristics. The challenge of making disciples should give us an added encouragement to monitor our own walk. Incidentally, there is still no suggestion in these passages that we should expect to model all gifts and skills. As we have already said in Chapter 1, only Jesus could do that.

COACHING QUESTIONNAIRE

This questionnaire is designed to help you analyse some of the principles and practices to do with coaching. Please score each of the following statements on a scale of 1 to 5. Five points indicates high agreement (you do these things well and regularly). One point signifies disagreement (this is rarely, if ever, your practice).

1. I watch other people doing things before I make any suggestions to them.

2. I can readily cope when strong emotions emerge in discipling sessions. ___

3. I am clear about my gifts. ___

4. Other people are prepared to admit to me that they may have a problem. ___

5. During discipling sessions I frequently summarise our progress. ___

6. I regularly find natural opportunities to help people develop. ___

7. I encourage people to take responsibility for their actions. ___

8. I understand the preferred pace of learning of those I am discipling. ___

9. I express the gifts that God has given me. ___

10. I help others get to the root of their problems, not just to the superficial symptoms. ___

11. I regularly involve other people in coaching opportunities when they are more gifted in the required areas. ___

12. I am willing to expose my own vulnerabilities to those I am coaching, if I think it will help.

13. Most months I put at least two hours into the specific development of each of those I coach.   ___

14. We start any discussion of an area for development with their thoughts and ideas, not mine.   ___

15. We agree clear boundaries and expectations throughout the coaching process.   ___

16. I help other people to complete the agreed course of action.   ___

17. I understand the need to generate a range of solutions, and regularly seek additional options.   ___

18. I understand the areas in which I am clearly not gifted and do not try to demonstrate them or teach about them.   ___

19. I listen actively by showing that I am listening.   ___

20. I quickly recognise when I am not the right person to help in a given situation.   ___

21. There is a mutually agreed action plan of goal outcomes from each session.   ___

22. I review our progress frequently and monitor our activity against our goals.   ___

23. I am generally optimistic about the ability of people to develop.   ___

24. I take the trouble to stay on top of any developments in my specialist fields.   ___

25. In the coaching context, I tackle problems rather than sweep them under the carpet.

   ___

26. When I am discipling, the other person will talk more than I do.

   ___

27. It is clear when my coaching input should come to a conclusion.

   ___

28. My diagnostic skills enable me to see where people are going wrong.

   ___

29. People I disciple have a good track record of going on to develop others.

   ___

30. I have a reputation for persistence, which others have found reliable.

   ___

31. I handle the complexity of relationship problems skilfully.

   ___

32. My advice is readily accepted.

   ___

33. Not only can I see where people are going wrong, but I see ways of putting things right.

   ___

34. I encourage a joint evaluation of our options.

   ___

35. I use my gifts for the edification of the whole body and in conjunction with those of others.

   ___

36. I celebrate other people's successes.

   ___

Add up your scores

for questions:	Total score	Facet of coaching indicated
6, 13, 15, 21, 22, 27		Appropriate structures
5, 12, 14, 19, 26, 32		Communication
4, 10, 17, 25, 31, 34		Problem-solving
3, 9, 18, 24, 29, 35		Understanding my own gifts
2, 7, 16, 23, 30, 36		Supporting
1, 8, 11, 20, 28, 33		Observation and analysis

I have broken down the components of coaching into six dimensions, shown in the right-hand column. The principal application of this questionnaire is to suggest that you work on just the two weakest scores; the strength of a chain is its weakest link and the effectiveness of your coaching will be hampered if your score in any of the ingredients is substantially lower than the others.

4

Mentoring

The origins of the word 'mentor' lie in Greek mythology. In Homer's *Odyssey*, Mentor was the highly respected servant of Ulysses, and among his other duties, the king entrusted to him the care and training of his own son, Telemacus. There was a wide range of aspects to this development, not only professional elements, but things like courage, character and attitudes.

This comprehensive approach to development is also recorded about the medieval trade guilds, where guild masters were responsible for social, religious and personal growth, as well as the technical components of the craft. The *Concise Oxford Dictionary* defines a mentor simply as an experienced and trusted adviser.

In the previous chapter we looked at coaching, and I want to continue to underline the differences between coaching and mentoring. We need an alternative approach to discipling in some situations, because we cannot coach in everything; we are not omni-competent! One of the gravest dangers in discipling is that when we cannot *show* people what to do, we usually *tell* them how to do it! I believe that this presumption has probably been the single biggest cause of our failure to disciple effectively, and the reason why most churches have not produced a disciple-making culture.

In the last chapter, we considered the principles and practice of coaching. Mentoring offers an alternative approach in areas we struggle to model. As a summary of the last chapter and an advance blueprint of this one, we can sum up the differences between coaching and mentoring in this table:

	Coaching	Mentoring
Focuses on:	Skill issues, technical shortfalls, and development opportunities	Attitudes, values and vision, and the whole person
Time scale:	Generally short term, and focusing on measurable results	Often sustained over a number of years
Approach based on:	Position, competence and demonstration	Relationship, trust, questions and offering perspective
Style:	Prescriptive and experiential	Non-directive and reflective
Outcomes:	Easily measured	Harder to define and measure

As I have been preparing this book, I've talked to many people. During discussions, we often reach the point of exploring the difference between a mentor and a spiritual director, a counsellor, a sponsor, a spiritual father/mother, or a soul friend.

Essentially, the debate can be largely academic. What matters is what we are doing, not what we call it. Terminology has been a great source of confusion. Different people will mean different things by identical terms, so we will always need to describe the relationship in more detail in order to understand the approach being taken. I have found it sufficient to use only two terms: coaching and mentoring. The above diagram describes the different characteristics of each. Discipling will often express varying mixtures with a blend of these two styles, and I have never known the outcome to be solely one or the other. The central theme in this book is that there are two principal arrows in the quiver called discipling, and we probably need to think about and practise the methods close to the extremes of each in order to strike the right balance and mixture more consistently.

If coaching assumes that the coach knows best and technically is more skilled than the disciple, mentoring is based on the following core functions and assumptions:

- The process is based on the relationship and trust.
- Listen and clarify as the disciple outlines the area for development.
- Help them to explore all possible facets of the problem.
- Present the disciple with the consequences of the possible solutions.
- Support them as they plan and take action.
- Work on the basis that they know best.
- Ask questions.

The key components of trust and asking questions that undergird mentoring are so important that they are given full chapters later in this book (Chapters 6 and 8). The problem of finding this balance between coaching and mentoring is not unique to the Christian sector and discipleship, so this is the right moment to see if the secular workplace has anything to teach us. Some companies have been running mentoring programmes for many years now and the better outcomes could show us some valid ideas about how to undertake discipleship. One general temptation applies to all mankind, and therefore both the Christian and business sectors. Out of motives that are at least partly pure, there is an over-readiness to give people advice that will enable them to short-cut the worst of our experiences. Nigel MacLennan, in his book *Coaching and Mentoring*, describes the problem this way:

> The performers you coach/mentor will probably be so used to being guided and taught that they may be shocked at the respect you wish to show them, and the trust you wish to assume in their abilities to achieve. How will you explain to them that you will not be directing them? How can you try to ensure that they don't see your non-directive approach as weakness and indecision?

The business world experiences the same difficulty with nomenclature as well. The words 'coach' and 'mentor' are commonly used, although probably the majority of recent secular literature has defined them in a complete reversal of the way that I have used the words! Other writers use the terms interchangeably. Again, the words can mean exactly what you want of them. Reg Hamilton describes the breadth of interpretation:

> Some mentoring relationships begin when senior people take an interest in, and promote the cause of, a subordinate or person they believe has untapped potential. Some people actively seek a mentor and approach another to help them learn. The result is

that the UK now has a wide range of approaches to mentoring, each with its own aims and consequent demands on mentors' experience and skills. (*Mentoring*, p. 7)

Some companies use the terms 'patron' or 'godfather' to describe the mentor, which implies a senior person. The benefits of family as an illustration of intimacy and sustained relationship are clearly realised by these organisations; they have acknowledged the power of a 'fathering' relationship. 'People who grew up in difficult circumstances and yet are successful have one thing in common; at a critical juncture in their adolescence, they had a positive relationship with a caring adult,' says Bill Clinton, quoted by Gareth Lewis in *Mentoring Manager* (p. viii). Then, using his own words, Lewis says, 'On one level I think mentoring is really trying to bring back some of the best elements of the extended family, but in a more formal way' (p. 99).

The relationship between God the Father and Jesus the Son is the ultimate model for the depth and intimacy of a mentor's approach. Obviously the relationship between a father and son is potentially much deeper than other friendships and Paul recognises the rarity of such quality: 'Even though you have ten thousand guardians in Christ, you do not have many fathers, for in Christ Jesus I became your father through the gospel' (1 Corinthians 4:15).

This sort of model is a privilege, and worth aspiring to. But I have to say that just as we have all seen good and bad parenting in blood families (let alone good and bad attitudes in children!), so it is in Christian discipling. As I have said before, we need to be less concerned about the label, and possibly its associated glamour, and more concerned with the quality of the relationship and the resultant fruit. Good mentors try to do the things that loving parents do: they care, encourage, direct, discipline and remain steadfast. When in doubt, we should look to the Godhead, who personifies all these qualities: 'Moreover, we have all had human fathers who disciplined us and we respected them for it. How much more should we submit to the Father of our spirits and live!' (Hebrews 12:9).

One consistent message comes from the workplace: you cannot mentor your immediate subordinates, because there would be role conflict. Every line manager has the responsibility to develop the staff who report to them, but the essence of line management denies some of the requirements for mentoring. When career progression is the main purpose of the mentoring relationship, some companies offer a mentor who is *two* levels above the learner's existing grade, and usually not directly in their part of the 'pyramid'. Your boss's boss is barely more suitable as a mentor than your boss – they are not dispassionate because they have a company agenda as well – but the possible benefits of being helped by somebody two levels above you are obvious. They have not just scraped a promotion from where you are; they have continued beyond. They must have been very successful at the intermediate level too. But there is no mystique to any of the roles. As Hamilton says about mentors: 'We are simply people who have probably experienced similar situations in the past' (p. 91).

We find that some functions of people development are nevertheless best undertaken by the line manager, and some are best detached in order to avoid role conflict. I am using the concept of the line manager unashamedly in the Christian forum; we can learn something from the parallels.

Opportunity	Description of developmental opportunity	Principal person responsible
Sponsorship	Opening doors. Having networks that will support development.	Both manager and mentor may be able to do this.
Coaching	Showing the ropes. Feedback and skill training to enhance effectiveness.	The job of a line manager. Day-to-day supervision is necessary.
Protection	Taking responsibility for mistakes outside their control. Acting as a buffer.	The line manager has to offer direct protection.
Exposure	Creating opportunities to demonstrate ability to those who matter. Enhancing profile and visibility.	Either can do this.
Challenging work	Delegating tasks and assignments that stimulate and stretch.	Central to a line manager's developmental role.
Role modelling	Demonstrating appropriate attitudes, behaviour and skills.	Both will be transmitting values all of the time, but are they the right ones?
Counselling	Providing a constructive, confidential forum to address aspirations and blockages.	Best done external to line management. The mentor can do this.
Acceptance	Support, affirmation, respect, resulting in strengthened confidence.	Both should be doing this all of the time; possible role conflict for manager.
Friendship	Caring beyond the job level. Sharing all parts of life.	Both manager and mentor. Easier for the mentor to go deeper.

The lessons from the business world are transferable: disciples need a range of inputs. If one person attempts to fill dual roles, the disciple potentially pays the price.

The qualities of a mentor

There are some core qualities in all proficient mentors, but some additional ones are necessary if they are going to be spiritually effective.

Mentors are spiritually mature

If they are going to contribute to enabling people to follow Jesus better, mentors must be people whose relationship with Jesus is meaningful and deep, and has been exposed to substantial challenges. Ideally, others should respect them in their faith, because they have a proven track record of faithfulness and of making disciples. Mentors have been 'round the block' in a spiritual sense, and experience tends to bring wisdom and knowledge (as well as just 'experience!'). Certainly the mentor must be compassionate and have the patience to both listen and wait for improvements, as some Christians increase in these characteristics quicker than others! Other personal spiritual qualities like discernment and the ability to confront are not always sufficiently developed in relatively new Christians.

However, we would be wrong to set the high jump bar too high. We all had to start somewhere! It's impossible to get a track record without initial experiences. Many people have served others magnificently by caring enough to listen, ask questions and be a sounding board. That's often the start of a mentoring discipling relationship.

Mentors point and lead disciples to God

It's one thing to commune with God and feed on what has been prepared for us in a personal way; it's quite another thing to help others to do the same for themselves. Helping people to appropriate the full message of grace is central to the work of discipling. We are called to offer love and acceptance to all because God has already done so. We need to be able to affirm all that God has already done for the disciple, and testify that God's faithfulness to his promises will guarantee the Spirit's continued work in the disciple's life.

Mentors will also be asked to help with questions of guidance, vision and direction from time to time. In the end, the disciple is responsible for their own long-term decisions and we must be careful not to be prescriptive and inadvertently impose our choices. Yet the good mentor is familiar with the ways of God and can sometimes recognise God's hallmark in a situation. Sometimes the real wisdom lies in the timing of sharing our views.

I had an unusual experience along these lines recently. A couple in a church where I work regularly were looking for another challenge. Their attitude was superb but their strengths were in personal evangelism, and the existing Alpha course was well resourced. I felt that they would be very fulfilled joining a church plant about thirty miles away; that would mean moving house but not changing jobs. One morning, I woke up certain that they should move, having had a really clear dream. This was something unique for me to experience as a form of guidance for others, and quite outside my usual style of thinking. For four months I waited until they contacted me about the possibility of moving and I was able to share the dream as a confirmation. Personally I would not have felt comfortable taking the initiative, because it might have been received as very prescriptive.

Mentors have a wholehearted belief in the disciple's potential and destiny

Just as Jesus recruited the disciples because he saw what they could become, so any mentor must have an unquenchable optimism about the future of the disciple. Jesus must have experienced many setbacks during the three years he trained them, yet he continued with them. One Christian said of his mentor: 'One of his hallmarks is his incredible passion to believe you into greatness. He never stops believing.'

There will be many periods without visible development when we need this passion about their future to keep us going as mentors. Here lies one of the benefits of the rule that discipling requires more than one contributor. On more than one occasion, as I have talked with the leader of my church about the development of specific individuals, we have reached a point where one of us has despaired about the lack of evident progress. Usually the other person saw things differently, or had sufficient resilience to persevere for longer at that time. Somebody has to retain optimism. It's a good barometer for me: if that spark is no longer there, there are major limitations to what I can contribute in the discipling process for a given individual. Effective mentoring is impossible. There is undoubtedly a spiritual dimension to this ability to see what people can become.

There is a final component to this boundless optimism about the potential of the disciple: it must be shockproof. From time to time, people will share deep sins and shortcomings with us that might cause us to fall off our chair in surprise. This sort of disclosure by the disciple is potentially very costly and high risk – for the individual and to the relationship – and at those times in particular we must retain unswerving confidence in their future.

Mentors have an empowering orientation

Nowadays we are all being constantly reminded as to what is politically correct in jargon and culture. For a season, the word 'empowerment' was almost being used in alternate sentences and was in danger of losing any true meaning. But in a real way, empowerment involves a genuine desire to seek to develop the potential in others, without dominating or having authority. It is part of both servant leadership and mentoring. The results of empowerment should be clearly visible: improved contributions, more ownership of the corporate agendas and a greater desire to experiment. The concept is not new; it's been around since Genesis chapter one.

I guess none of us does anything out of totally pure motives in this life and we should not wait for ever before commencing discipleship. Nevertheless, there is a real danger of helping others primarily to gratify a need in ourselves. As I heard one speaker say recently, we should present our bodies as a living sacrifice, but on whose altar? There are probably two acid tests that will expose our motives: how much do we want the credit and how much are we prepared to do that which is unseen? True empowerment and discipleship are not about personal gratification or public profile. It's interesting how Paul talks about the work he did with the Thessalonian church:

> You are witnesses, and so is God, of how holy, righteous and blameless we were among you who believed. For you know that we dealt with each of you as a father deals with his own children, encouraging, comforting and urging you to live lives worthy of

God, who calls you into his kingdom and glory. (1 Thessalonians 2:10–12, following the mothering component in verse 7)

The verbs that Paul associates with fathering are 'encouraging', 'comforting' and 'urging'. The first verb speaks of giving courage, and the second is more strident than we usually identify with comfort (from the Latin *cum forte*, meaning 'with strength'). All three verbs offer a dimension of forward movement.

Mentors have an accurate self-awareness

We will talk much more about this subject in Chapter 7, but there is one big area of self-awareness that is critical for mentors. They must be pretty accurate in their assessment of their own active, legitimate coaching repertoire. *The good mentor recognises the range of skills where their own shortfalls mean that they should not coach*, and will put disciples in touch with other mentors and coaches from time to time. However, because of the depth of the relationship, and perhaps a responsibility for oversight of the discipling process, the mentor will continue to monitor the disciple's development, asking how the training is going, encouraging the disciple and being ready to be more available after a skill has been consolidated.

Mentors are objective and neutral

This is the prime reason why the manager cannot be a mentor. The manager's role is complicated by responsibility to the organisation for the performance and results delivered by the subordinate. The manager is not neutral in the way that a detached mentor can be.

A manager may also be responsible for more than one

person, so they cannot offer increased opportunities to every-body. A mentor needs to be able to offer neutrality. In my own work, leaders from a wide variety of churches, missions and charities come to see me about their own development. Often I will meet no other person from their organisation, so I am seen as external with no personal axe to grind (except that often the organisation pays my fee!). Discipling within my own church is often harder. Confidentiality issues are more vulnerable; they have seen my weaknesses, and my passion for the whole church could be at odds with the needs of any given member.

The objectivity of the mentor does not prevent them from giving factual feedback, but this is more commonly the role of the coach. Mentors often act as sounding boards, to help the disciple think through the issues and come to their own con-clusions. Above all, mentors must be non-judgemental, and perhaps a shoulder to cry on.

Mentors must be vulnerable and open

Paul writes to Timothy: 'You, however, know all about my teaching, my way of life, my purpose, faith, patience, love, endurance, persecutions, sufferings – what kinds of things happened to me in Antioch, Iconium and Lystra, the persecu-tions I endured' (2 Timothy 3:10).

We must be prepared to share our own experiences, weak-nesses and failings. I think that this is one possible distinction between mentoring and certain extreme approaches to coun-selling; you cannot build a relationship with a blank wall or a paragon of virtue. An artificially robust and inaccurate self-presentation cripples progress. The disciple will be deterred from being open, and ultimately the fruit will be unreality and deception. Wise, timely disclosures produce respect and do not actually encourage people to walk all over you, which is the commonly held fear.

Mentors are committed

Perhaps one of the greatest limitations to mentoring is availability. Real growth in disciples requires availability for the long haul. One good friend whom I mentor has just changed jobs, becoming a chief executive for the first time. Much of my work with him has been around his career development over a period of three years, identifying and organising experiences to make him ready for such a position. Mentoring him had not proved to be time intensive, but suddenly, with the new job, many immediate issues were raised: self-doubts, upheaval for the family, etc. The timing was not good for me, but that's what mentoring is about. He is going to be an excellent CEO, although he doesn't believe it yet!

Because of time pressures, one of the greatest dangers for new mentors is to rush through the early stages of relationship-building in order to try to produce quick results. It takes time to develop trust, intimacy and confidentiality, but these are the foundational elements of relationships that produce quality, long-lasting fruit.

Questions

* Who has been a mentor for you in the past?
* Who fills this role for you now?
* What are the qualities that you respect in them?

5

The Process of Discipling

When I visit churches and work with leadership teams, I am often asked for a route map to see discipling widely implemented. There has been a clear recognition that discipling is biblical, that people want to see it enhanced, and that there is very little of it present in many churches at the moment. Whilst this might sound a pretty depressing situation, it is by far the most common that I encounter. The questions that leaders are asking regarding how to get going are typically accompanied by some humorous banter like, 'I know. If you were us, you wouldn't start from here.' As with most major changes and initiatives, the timing and present circumstances never seem to be ideal.

Starting discipling

Without doubt, the key requirement is a group of people who want to disciple and who want to be discipled. The desire to be discipled is a good qualification and criterion for people who offer their services as coaches or mentors. Jesus submitted himself to the authority of the Father in all he did; it was the foundation of every act. Based on this, we should be concerned about any attempt by people to put themselves in a position 'over' other people if they are not prepared to come 'under'. Please set this hierarchical language in the wider context of what we said in Chapter 2 about how relationships are the basis of discipleship and that we all need more than one input.

Just as the timing of any initiative is seldom perfect, so there are issues of numerical support. What percentage of the membership must be on board before we can set sail? Well, don't wait for 100 per cent! As the profile and credibility of discipling is enhanced, so more people will want to take part. Success breeds success, usually by gossiping about it. There should be a twin approach to gaining support. Draw in existing members who say that they want to be involved. Additionally, make sure that new members, especially those who come from an unchurched background, are introduced to the discipling process from the beginning of their Christian life. It's important that they quickly come to understand that discipleship is the normal Christian life. Whether you have a newcomers' course, a membership class, or even confirmation preparation, this is the time to implant this value. If both approaches work well, then you have a diminishing population who are not involved. New members are often more responsive, especially if they have joined the church by a 'friendship evangelism' method; these people have proved much easier to disciple.

In any church structure the leadership must check that certain conditions have been met before embarking on such a radical change as the widespread adoption of discipling. The following questions give a guide to the readiness of the church:

1. Is the church both ready and capable? What else must be achieved before starting out? The Israelites were asked to do some strange things before setting out for the Promised Land. Sometimes churches have some untouched business to attend to before launching a discipling process. Lack of vision, the wrong culture (and we'll define the 'right' culture later, in Chapter 14) and unresolved conflicts are examples of issues that might prevent a gathering of momentum.

2. Have the aims and goals of discipleship been defined? Chapter 13 might give you some indications.

3. Is there a commitment from the top, and is this visible? The credibility of any change or initiative is decidedly low if the leaders have not embraced the decision and practice individually for themselves.

4. What are the criteria for selecting mentors and for selecting disciples? Often the small group leader may have a role to play in recommending people who are ready to disciple. Ultimately we want everybody to be involved.

5. What is the system for matching mentors and disciples? When discipleship begins, personal choice is probably sufficient, but as greater numbers are involved, some co-ordination and allocation is probably needed. Folk like to be clear on who does this matching and on what basis.

6. What training will be given to both parties? The skill of questioning is crucial to mentoring. Other training that I have seen in churches provides quality assurance. If we want people who can disciple families, help job seekers or teach some basic church history, training may involve providing materials and sharing knowledge. The coaches and mentors may need resources; we may need manuals to cover the core materials for the disciples.

7. Have terms of reference been set and guidelines given? Boundaries provide security for all parties.

8. What are the systems in place for monitoring and evaluating the process? If question 2 has not been answered properly, the process will be impossible to evaluate. Criteria and methodology have to be established at the outset. Against what will we evaluate?

9. What are the contingency plans to deal with problems? With the best will in the world, some combinations of coach/mentor and disciple will be judged by both parties to have failed. Ideally leaders, in a wide sense of the word, should be able to check that every effort has been made within the relationship and be able to provide alternative combinations.

10. Have all of the above been communicated to all those involved? All the above criteria should be in place, but that's not enough. Change brings uncertainty and the best antidote to uncertainty is communication. Tell as many people as you can, as much as you can, as soon as you can.

In considering the early stages of a discipling initiative, there is a danger of wanting to produce quick results. Remember that discipling is both relational and purposeful. I've usually found that we need to invest heavily in the relationship at this time, especially if mentoring is going to be the outcome. The bridge of trust may only have been tested to low limits up to now, so tread carefully.

After some initial progress and adoption

(a) The right frequency

The parties must agree on the frequency of meeting. I'm often asked for my recommendations about this, and the answer depends on the purpose and expectations of those in the relationship. I have coached people to manage their financial affairs better and the first meeting has been triggered by a crisis, like impending legal action. Sometimes meetings have been twice weekly, or at least one meeting plus one telephone call, until we have staved off the immediate crisis. In some formal mentoring relationships, I have regular, structured quarterly meetings. That schedule has proved sufficient, bearing in mind that most of us see change in only a few major areas in any one year. In local church mentoring patterns, I have found monthly contacts to be about right. Much as in counselling, there is an optimum duration of about an hour and a half per session. The temptation is to go for fewer, longer meetings. That's understandable, because every meeting involves travel time and a little ice-breaking and catching up, but is not advisable. Longer meetings tend to become heavy, have fewer opportunities for actioning issues and tend to go over the same ground repeatedly.

(b) Documentation

Over the years my work has included considerable exposure to the world of residential care, in training the managers of residential homes. Happily there is a considerable Christian presence in this service and ministry. Some of the formal procedures of the social services' work are wise. All staff members are expected to have a 'supervision' session with their line manager about once every six weeks. These sessions are accompanied by formal record-keeping. At one time, paper-work for staff development lagged behind the client develop-ment plan, which had a similar purpose. But if we can have a development plan for clients, then why not for staff? The answer very clearly was that staff development was seen as less important than client development. In discipling, I maintain brief notes of all meetings. Referring to them adds focus to the next meeting, and promotes continuity and accountability, as well as preventing an action replay! Generally I use two colours in my note-making: one to summarise what was said and the other to record my personal reflections and provi-sional conclusions.

Years ago, when I played chess to a decent standard, one book had an impact on my play more than any other. It was called *My System* and was written by Aron Nimzowitsch. In many ways the principles he propagated were neither new nor revolutionary; the benefit of reading the book was that I applied the principles more frequently, because he had brought them from the subconscious to the conscious mind. Some limited documentation of discipleship meetings offers the same advantage: we are more likely to do what we have logged.

(c) Expectations

This is a tricky one, since there are bound to be variations within the broad swathe of the process of discipling. Yet we must be aware that some people have unrealistically high expectations and others are tempted to produce a climate that is too cosy. Chapter 13 is designed to help you think about the outcomes of discipling. The nature of the relationship and dynamics should change over a period of time, with the increased maturity of both parties. My coach in the 1980s in

Christian leadership training was so far ahead of me that the relationship was all but totally one-sided! Over many years the dynamics have become much more two-way.

(d) Resources and materials

Herein, to my mind, lies one of the biggest single pitfalls in the process of producing a discipling mentality. Hopefully as the process takes off, more people will want to be involved. The initial training may well have finished. Newer enthusiasts are likely to be less skilled. The support provided by the leaders is spread more thinly. There is a great temptation to resolve these problems by becoming heavily reliant on written materials such as manuals, equipping tracks, courses and programmes. Patterns of discipling in the New Testament are conspicuously lacking in these things! The main characteristics were relationships, to the level of sharing lives. This is widely visible in Paul's writing, as well as in the gospels. Remember, discipling is a process, not a programme. There are times of rapid expansion when guidelines are necessary and a flexible programme is useful, but the danger lies in trying to impose too much detail. As we said earlier, discipling does not seek to produce a 'one size fits all' tee-shirt!

Variations in style

I have noticed six key dimensions that illustrate contrasts in discipling styles. The ends of the dimensions are summarised in the diagram on page 76. Note that there is no structure to the two columns (that is to say, the left- and right-hand columns in isolation are making no attempt to represent a single approach).

Top-down and one-way	Two-way
Leader led	Member led
Directive	Non-prescriptive
Individualistic/personal	Group work, plus one-to-one sessions
Formal	A mixture of formal and informal
Ad hoc	Planned

I am strongly advocating that an effective style will emphasise the right-hand side of the diagram. Historically churches have favoured some ingredients of the left side, assuming that trained people have something worth teaching. My experience is that discipling should be two-way, but that the relationship is not about equal partners. The coach/mentor can potentially learn many things from the process, but it will be quite clear who is discipling whom. The danger of top-down discipling is that the process comes to rely on position, not relationship. For all members to disciple as well as to receive is simply justified in the light of the Great Commission.

I believe that many discipling relationships are too directive. Throughout this book I am favouring two approaches, which I've called coaching and mentoring; my descriptions have been polarised and distinctive. In practice, over a period of time, the chosen style will be more intermingled. That's good.

Again, from my own limited experience and observations, discipling has sometimes drifted to being too close to counselling. There are grave dangers, as we have said, of possessiveness and exposure to only one input. The pressures of time have also encouraged some to try to disciple a group simultaneously. The problem at this end of the axis is that the development does not take sufficient account of individuality.

The last two boxes are easily understood. Again, if I am asked about dangers and preferences, I tend towards the informal/deliberate approach. We're in a serious business, but sessions shouldn't be 'heavy' for the sake of it.

Ending

During our time on this earth, discipleship should never end. It's a lifestyle and a biblical mandate. But from time to time, certain combinations of coach/mentor and disciple should come to a close. It's simplest to consider the criteria for finishing in each of the two types of relationship, coaching and mentoring.

Coaching is likely to have a shorter life-span than mentoring, but it is often more intense. As soon as the skill or life feature has been acquired from the modelling of the coach, then it is legitimate to come to a close. In practice, this isn't always the case. Sometimes a high trust level develops during the coaching and both parties want to retain not only the friendship, but a purpose as well. Coaching will often end up touching attitudes, including the emotional barriers to development. For these reasons, what was assumed to be a coaching relationship with a limited expectation of time frame sometimes blossoms to become a mentoring relationship.

It is harder to know when a mentoring relationship should close down. Often they do break down before the potential has been maximised. It's more likely to be the disciple who calls a halt to the process. Here are some of the negative reasons that I've known:

- A breach of trust by the mentor.
- The mentor becomes too directive in areas where the disciple is uncomfortable.
- The disciple becomes disappointed with the competence of the mentor.
- One party breaks the boundaries that were established at the beginning.
- The relationship becomes tarnished by possessiveness and exclusivity.
- The relationship is too dependent on resources and they have expired.

Sometimes I've known people continue the mentoring relationship for too long, out of a sense of duty and not wanting to have failed. We need to remember that often there will be a natural end; the spark has gone and the chemistry isn't there any more. This sort of tired feeling is a typical symptom of time for a change.

On the positive side, there may be better and more natural reasons for an end to a mentoring relationship. The disciple may have moved away geographically, or they may have grown to a level of maturity that requires a different mentor (to the lasting credit of the existing person in that role). Major changes in health or life may demand different inputs. There are many good reasons why a change of mentor may suit all parties and be appropriate.

6

Trust

Trust sets the limits of discipling

Gone are the old days when trust was automatically given to traditional authority figures. Schoolteachers no longer receive respect and trust just because of their function or position; it has got to be earned. Ministers, other people in church leadership positions, coaches and especially mentors are pretty much in the same category. In some ways it's not altogether a bad thing that the dynamics and status are less prescribed and guaranteed. There's a greater emphasis on relationship and less of an emphasis on position; in the long run, the new rationale will be more effective.

Trust is obviously important in the business of mentoring. It's the oxygen of human relationships at all levels, including marriages, families and churches, so it is critical that those folk who seek to disciple others earn and understand trust. Every mentoring relationship has a plateau that is determined by the level of mutual trust. Any meeting can increase or decrease this key factor. Yet for some time, as I've mulled over the

subject of trust, read about it and observed successful discipling relationships, I've still found the components hard to
define and identify. What are the basic constituents of trust?
What do they depend on? How and why does trust grow or
diminish? Is it about who we are or what we do? A couple of
years ago, I felt the issue was so important that I invested all
my reading time for about six months into the subject of trust.
That period probably initiated this chapter and that reading
encouraged me to use more quotations than usual.

In the armed forces, in leadership teams, indeed in any situation requiring interdependence, the need for trust is fairly
self-evident. In mentoring, trust is particularly important
because the team is so small – two people sharing intimate
information. The consequences of *not* being prepared to trust
can be very serious:

An Air Florida aircraft waits on the runway of National Airport,
Washington DC, one winter evening. Conditions are bad. Despite
the best efforts of the airport de-icing team, there are still icicles
hanging from the wings of the aircraft. The co-pilot repeatedly
draws the pilot's attention to this, but does so in a tentative
manner, like many co-pilots, because he does not want to appear
to challenge his senior officer's judgement. Equally, the pilot evi-
dently does not trust the judgement of his second-in-command.
The last words recorded on the black box flight recorder are those
of the pilot, dismissing his co-pilot's comments about icicles.
Shortly afterwards the plane attempts to take off, but ice on the
wings causes it to crash into the Potomac River. All but 5 of the
74 people on board are killed. Their lives would have been saved
if there had been more trust on the flight deck. (Larry Reynolds,
The Trust Effect, p. 3)

The trustworthiness of God

Just as we looked in Chapter 1 at Jesus as a model for making disciples, so in order to begin to understand trustworthiness, we must start by looking at God. The Old Testament is the account of God establishing covenant with his people and remaining faithful to his promises, even though the other party regularly breaks the deal. There are at least twenty references in Genesis, and eleven in Exodus, to 'covenant'. The New Testament is about the message of grace, and a new relationship, which permanently covers our fallibility. Only recently, I was struck by the fact that I am saved by the blood of Christ but in a way kept for God by his own faithfulness to his promises. Where would I be if he tore up the agreement that he instituted? I could have no other plea. Here is a very small sample of the verses that assure us of God's faithful and trustworthy nature.

'I will establish my covenant as an everlasting covenant between me and you and your descendants after you for the generations to come, to be your God and the God of your descendants after you.' (Genesis 17:7)

The Lord, the Lord, the compassionate and gracious God, slow to anger, abounding in love and faithfulness, maintaining love to thousands, and forgiving wickedness, rebellion and sin. (Exodus 34:6–7)

Know therefore that the Lord your God is God; he is the faithful God, keeping his covenant of love to a thousand generations of those who love him and keep his commands. (Deuteronomy 7:9)

'As I was with Moses, so I will be with you; I will never leave you nor forsake you . . . For the Lord your God will be with you wherever you go.' (Joshua 1:5, 9)

Then I said: 'O Lord, God of heaven, the great and awesome God, who keeps his covenant of love with those who love him and obey his commands . . .' (Nehemiah 1:5)

Those who know your name will trust in you, for you, Lord, have never forsaken those who seek you. (Psalm 9:10)

The works of his hands are faithful and just; all his precepts are trustworthy. (Psalm 111:7)

Jesus Christ is the same yesterday, and today and for ever. (Hebrews 13:8)

Not only can we rely on his character, but we can also rely on the fact that he is able to do what he says he is going to do.

He provided redemption for his people; he ordained his covenant for ever – holy and awesome is his name. (Psalm 111:9)

And God is able to make all grace abound to you, so that in all things at all times, having all that you need, you will abound in every good work. (2 Corinthians 9:8)

Now to him who is able to do immeasurably more than all we ask or imagine . . . (Ephesians 3:20)

To him who is able to keep you from falling and to present you before his glorious presence without fault and with great joy . . . (Jude 24)

Perhaps the best summary of God's trustworthiness is found in the names of God (Jehovah) in the Old Testament:

Name	Reference	Meaning
Jireh	Genesis 22:14	The Lord our provider
Rapha	Exodus 15:26	The Lord our healer
Nissi	Exodus 17:15	The Lord our banner
Mikaddesh	Exodus 31:13	The Lord our sanctifier
Shalom	Judges 6:24	The Lord our peace
Ramah	Psalm 23:1	The Lord our shepherd
Tsidkenu	Jeremiah 23:6	The Lord our righteousness
Shammah	Ezekiel 48:35	The Lord is present

It would be easy to feel overwhelmed rather than encouraged by this list of scriptures and names, but that's not the object of the exercise! As mentors, we have an additional responsibility to yearn to be more Christ-like; he is totally trustworthy and we seek to become more trustworthy than we are. In essence, the more we become like him, the more we can be trusted.

Trustworthiness is a function of both character and competence. Character is about how we behave; competence is more about the required capability in a given role.

Character

Let's look first at the ingredients of character found in the type of people who are trustworthy. There will be some similarity between this list and the qualities of a good mentor in Chapter 4: I want to analyse them in greater depth and highlight the impact that these qualities have on trustworthiness. I suggest that the key components of trustworthiness are:

Consistency

There can be no major fluctuations in lifestyle or emotional mood swings. Jesus was far from predictable but he modelled the core qualities of acceptance and joy perfectly to his disciples. Church members today also expect their mentors to offer a consistent welcome. Whatever surprises we may face ourselves, they must not spill over into how we receive other people. A good leader is equally approachable on Monday morning or on Friday afternoon. This is not to say that good mentors are devoid of emotion; Jesus shared his surprises, pleasures and grief.

Congruency

We must walk the talk. Gaps between what we teach and what we live destroy credibility very quickly. Real values will be caught from our lives, not from our teaching. Modelling is still the loudest message at the disposal of a mentor. Theories that we hold but don't live out haven't got much to commend them. The key to congruency is that the different roles in our lives are approached in the same way. Once you have met me, whether it was first at home, in a seminar or at the cricket club, then there should be no surprises if you later meet me in a different context. Identity (how I see myself) and image (how

I am seen) ought to match as well. It is also disconcerting to potential disciples if the view of self varies dramatically from time to time. Generally this would indicate a rather low personal worth bolstered by flashes of arrogance. The lowest indicator of self-worth may well be the closest to the truth.

Integrity

Integrity is like a multi-faceted crystal: there are many aspects and shades to the meaning. It certainly encompasses all that honesty contains, but much more as well. People with integrity say what they mean and mean what they say. Their word is their bond; they honour their commitments and promises. Integrity contains measures of wholeness and completeness. In *Developing the Leader within You* Maxwell says, 'Integrity means living it myself before leading others' (p. 42). There must also be transparency – an openness, like a pane of glass, to being understood. This is slightly, but importantly, different from vulnerability.

Supportiveness

When the chips are really down, mentors will be there for people, and dependable. The challenges they offer will seldom exceed the available care. Sometimes the expectations of disciples misunderstand the nature of support: I have had such an experience recently. I fundamentally disagreed with a course of action that some friends were pursuing. The issue involved values, not just life choices. They mistook my disagreement for a lack of support. They did not understand that I would be there for them, through thick and thin, whatever the consequences. My support was (and is), unconditional, even though they did not have my agreement.

Sometimes support is best evidenced by listening, no more

and no less. Don Payne suggests that listening may be an expression of something deeper:

> Trust grows out of humility. When a person does not presume to know what's in my head and is willing to hear me out, that engenders trust. I tend to hold at a distance people who seem to make prejudgements about what I need or what I need to hear. (*Leadership* magazine, Spring 2000, p. 39)

Reliability

Values are evidenced by repetitions of behaviour. Each isolated incident can be seen as trivial in its own right, but a host of similar events can make a big impression between them. The pattern eventually makes a statement about values. I had an A-level maths teacher who personified this: if he said that our exercise books would be returned on Thursday, then they were. He was consistently punctual, and expected the same from us. Recently I heard a negative example about a church leader – that he was negligent in returning phone calls. The trait had begun to have a negative effect on members. Reliability is close to faithfulness, and the ultimate message is about how much we care.

Competence

Over the last decade, the business world has defined competence in a broader sense than previously. Competence can be seen as a cluster of attitudes, skills and behaviours which are essential to high performance in the role. Competence can reinforce or destroy trust just as much as character can. Good character does not guarantee that trust is accorded.

The story is told of a man who lived in a small rural community. He went to the doctor with a knee problem. The doctor was a very fine person, popular and liked around the village. However, as a doctor, he was at best a very general practitioner, with some significant technical weaknesses. The minor work that he undertook on the knee was not sufficient to solve the cruciate ligament problem and the patient was left with a permanent, though slight, limp. Unfortunately there seemed to be a hereditary element to the problem and later the man's children began to show similar symptoms. The doctor's character was excellent, but they did not regard him as trustworthy because they didn't think that he was competent as a doctor.

As roles become more demanding, competent people must be committed to remaining up to date with the necessary skills and behaviours; competence is not a static standard. One CEO put the requirement this way: 'Now I understand for the first time why I don't trust some people. I think, "You're a good person. You're honest. So why don't I trust you?" I realise now it's because they're not competent. They haven't stayed current in their profession. They're obsolete. They've been carried by the organisation. They don't have the spirit of continuous improvement.' Reynolds phrases the expectation very starkly: 'People remain competent only if they are committed to learning. Without learning there is no competence; without competence, there is no trust' (*The Trust Effect*, pp. 169, 171).

We can develop trust in very practical ways. It's rather like a joint bank account. Both parties need to make deposits regularly into the mutual kitty. Every confidence kept, every piece of advice that works, every moment of humour enjoyed together – these are the sorts of positive experience that add to the balance in the account. Trustworthiness creates flexibility and emotional reserves in relationships. Minor misunderstandings erode the balance in the account. Occasionally, however, one of the parties might make a serious mistake. If there are sufficient reserves in the account to draw on and meet the demand, the relationship will not be deemed bankrupt by either party. However, if relational bankruptcy occurs, it is more likely to be permanent than temporary; trust, once truly severed, is very hard to re-establish. Remember that the account is in the joint names of the mentor and the disciple. We can do things that have the potential to build up trust, but we cannot guarantee how an action will be perceived. Trust cannot be acquired; it can only be given or accorded to us. Mentoring without mutual trust is a contradiction in terms.

Undoubtedly there are two principal methods of building trust. One way of generating trust is to be found to be trust-worthy; the other is to give trust. Trust resides squarely between faith and doubt. It is founded on the expectation that others will prove trustworthy. People will let us down from time to time, but as mentors we still need to lead in being pre-pared to put the first instalment in the kitty. God trusted people right from Genesis chapter one, not merely taking risks, but knowing that they and all mankind would make a mess of things. In verse 28 we see that immediately after being created, mankind was given the rule over every creature.

It is important to understand that trust is given and received to different degrees in different issues. For example, in general terms my wife Vicky trusts me. But that broad statement hides a much more complex charter! She trusts me to handle the family finances astutely; that would be seen as one of my strengths. Every day that I leave home to go to work, she trusts me not to run off with the prettiest female delegate at the con-ference (or perhaps she is just confident that they are more dis-cerning!). But in other areas her trust levels are far lower. I am not to be trusted in secondhand bookshops; the track record is that I seldom come away empty-handed. The ultimate challenge came recently when I started some very basic plumbing under the kitchen sink, and her face conveyed very clearly that she was not anticipating a successful outcome! A defensive response would be, 'Huh, so you don't trust me then?' How often have we had that said to us? Vicky's reply could legitimately have been, 'In many respects, comprehensively, but not in this particular area of plumbing.' Beware when people generalise from the particular.

The implications of this section for disciplers, coaches and mentors are far-reaching. Being of good character is not sufficient to generate trust. We also need to be competent in the agreed role, and committed to remaining so.

The wise use of information

How we share information with disciples can enhance trust or be quite destructive of it. It's easy to look for the short-term gain in the way we handle information, without realising that the longer term consequences may be significantly negative. If we are reluctant to reveal sensitive information and make disclosures about individuals, then it can seem that we are retaining knowledge as part of a power game; being 'in the know' is a sign of prestige. Sharing things too quickly gives a superficial indication that we trust the person, but soon their minds begin to be suspicious, and rightly so. If Y initially feels trusted because we share information and negative comments about X with them, then soon Y will assume that we will share their revelations in turn with others as well. As soon as they recognise that possibility, trust plummets. Peterson and Hicks summarise the long-term costs well:

The temptation to bring people into your confidence by sharing insider information or criticising others can be very compelling. The short-term gain is often a feeling of special trust with your confidant. But when you share confidences or criticisms with people, you ultimately erode their willingness to share their vulnerability, weaknesses and concerns with you.' (*Leader as Coach*, p. 43)

It would be wise to apply this checklist before sharing information:

- Does sharing this information breach a confidence?
- How sensitive is this information to their feelings and values?
- How will this information help them, either in their understanding or in their behaviour?
- When will be the most appropriate time to share this information?
- Is this sharing designed to help them or to enhance my position in regard to them?

A good additional criterion to use in deciding whether to share information or not is to ask: 'Are the interests of those who aren't present both respected and protected by sharing this information?' If the answer is 'No', then don't share!

QUESTIONNAIRE

Please score each of the following twenty statements. Give 3 points if a statement is always true for you, 2 points if it is often true, 1 point if it is sometimes true, and 0 points if it is seldom true.

1. I am well known as a person who delivers what I promise.

___

2. My track record in the field of discipling is well established.

___

3. At any given time, I have goals linked to my own personal development.

___

4. The people I disciple are extremely confident that I will represent them positively in their absence.

___

5. I have a track record of supporting people during their difficult times.

___

6. People generally say that sessions with me are focused and worthwhile.

___

7. Other people know that I do not break confidences.

___

8. I regularly take time out from the normal routine of work for my own development.

___

9. People say that I wear my heart on my sleeve.

___

10. I am generally very optimistic about the potential of other people.

___

11. When I share information, it's not to improve my own image.

___

12. I readily adapt my discipling style to take account of the individual disciple.

___

13. I am known for 'walking the talk'.

___

14. I am sensitive about feelings and timing when I reveal information.

___

15. My diagnostic skills surrounding people development are well honed.

___

16. I have helped the most unlikely people to take great strides forward.

            ___

17. When I express a range of emotions, people still know that I love them.

            ___

18. There is always a positive purpose when I share information.

            ___

19. I take great delight in making a contribution to the progress of other people.

            ___

20. I have wide experience of discipling different people in different situations.

            ___

Add up your scores for questions:	Total score	Quality assessed in this cluster
1, 5, 9, 13, 17		Character
2, 6, 12, 15, 20		Competence as a discipler
3, 8, 10, 16, 19		Commitment to development
4, 7, 11, 14, 18		Wise use of information

This questionnaire seeks to identify the qualities of a trustworthy person. It's not a case of playing to strengths and ignoring weaknesses – we need all of the qualities. Analyse the questions that contributed to your lowest total and work on that feature. Trust is very fragile and no score should be lower than nine. You might like to get a second opinion on your self-assessment by asking somebody else to score this questionnaire, treating you as the subject.

7

Strengths and Weaknesses

The triggers for this chapter came thick and fast during the winter months a few years ago. I sat on various interviewing panels and also happened to conduct some training courses on appraisals. The same question kept cropping up time and again: 'What are your strengths and weaknesses?' What really caught my attention was the lack of exploration that followed the question, and in most cases the absence of any benefit to the whole process. About that time, I gave a reference for a friend who was applying for a job. (Before I complete the story I hasten to add that he did get the job!) I was asked the same old question, and on the telephone I replied that the candidate knew nothing whatsoever about Chinese pottery. A dry chuckle confirmed my hopes that this did not necessarily rule out the candidate. A better question might have been: 'What strengths and weaknesses would be significant factors contributing to the person's ability to do this job?'

Other examples of poor use of the original question ('What are your strengths and weaknesses?') crossed my path around the same time and compounded my interest in possibly improving the wording and applications. I undertake a fair amount of management training for senior staff in residential care centres and the social services sector has its own terminology and definitions of good practice. All members of staff are expected to have a semi-formal meeting with their line manager roughly once every six weeks, typically for about forty-five minutes. This meeting, called 'a supervision', is more common in this sector as a development tool than the annual appraisal. The increased frequency has considerable advantages but, as we have already said in earlier chapters, there won't be major changes in mature staff across six-week periods, hence the record forms often repeatedly commented on the same weaknesses. Sometimes the real problem lay in the lack of an action plan. Nevertheless, the typical outcome was often demoralising and always demotivating.

As a result of the challenges presented by these events, I devised the table shown below. I have used it frequently in discipling sessions, generally discussing its application with the disciple, but occasionally just using it as a diagnostic tool within my own thinking. The shape of the table is based on one key principle:

DIFFERENT TYPES OF WEAKNESS REQUIRE VERY DIFFERENT RESPONSES

In the table, I have focused on devising an action plan for addressing weaknesses rather than strengths; that's the more common application. The role or job makes demands on the individual and exposes shortcomings, which are worked on via the discipling session. The debatable assumption is that roles are deemed less flexible than people! I have also used the thinking behind the table in a parallel approach, looking at how to maximise the opportunities for releasing strengths,

HANDLING WEAKNESSES

Feature	Weaknesses	Possible positive responses	Goal	Action
Character issues (Galatians 5:22)		God Self-discipline Pastoral care		
Skills and competencies		Training Coaching Practice		
Motive profile Achievement Affiliation Power		Spot the temptation Manage it Resist it		
Team roles (Belbin's roles)		You can't be good at everything. Work in a team		
Knowledge		Learning Studying Research		
Emotional competence		Journalling Staying in touch with your emotions		

sometimes in 'career progression' thinking. The same mentality deserves to be used more often in the church, looking for
further opportunities to express gifts, because although the
idea of a 'career' is rather alien, the concept of pilgrimage is
not. The table will serve as a framework for this chapter and
we will analyse all the terms and components.

Let's look at each of these features in turn.

Character issues

Character proves to be the broadest of my list of types of
weakness containing many possible strands, and often the
most difficult to pinpoint. Generally, these weaknesses also
prove to be the most critical, for whereas skill and knowledge
deficiencies can delay entry to leadership positions for a while,
character weaknesses can prevent such opportunities for ever.
Additionally, we often find that the root of other problems
that we initially identified to be in other features are actually
to be found in the character realm.

I have suggested in the diagram that the fruit of the Spirit,
as listed in Galatians 5:22 (love, joy, peace, patience, kindness,
goodness, faithfulness, gentleness and self-control), forms
a good basis for an assessment of 'good character'. In
Mentoring to Develop Disciples and Leaders (p. 57), Mallison
lists the following twelve major character-related areas of life
that deserve attention because he has found that people are
frequently vulnerable in them:

• friendships
• spouse and family
• self-centredness
• pride, self-image

- lust
- honesty
- power
- acknowledgement of authority
- servanthood
- availability for service
- greed, attitude towards money
- time management

I'm in close to 100 per cent agreement with his list, and more importantly they are all character-related – even time management, since it reflects our priorities. Character is like an overlay that blankets personality and gifts. When we mature and progress in character, it is reflected in everything else.

How do we make progress in our lives in the dimensions of character? I'm suggesting three ways that I've seen frequently, although I'm sure there are many others. First, there is no substitute for a direct encounter with God. It might be through a passage in our devotional time, a moment of conviction, or a Spirit-prompted realisation that there is a plank in our own eye just as we are about to criticise somebody else! Second, we should not belittle the importance of self-discipline. Often when people say 'can't', they really mean 'won't', a matter of volition. We can choose the better path every time we come to the crossroads.

The third contribution to our progress in character development relies on the help of other people – the principle of iron sharpening iron. Broadly, I've labelled this concept as pastoral care. The assistance may come from a coach or mentor, pastor or minister, but some of the most durable improvements I have experienced and observed are down to the influence of friends and peers.

I've written extensively in a previous book (*Small Group Know How*) about pastoral care, as I believe the weight of New Testament evidence radically challenges the culture in many churches in respect of this area of life. There are over fifty references to 'one anothering' (the principle that we care for each other) and about thirteen to 'shepherd', many of which can clearly only refer to Jesus. Pastoral care is the responsibility of the whole flock, not just the few, although some may have particular gifts in this field. Rubbing the rough edges off each other, for example in the small group setting, often produces sustained fruit in our lives; the hurly-burly of everyday life is a good teacher. Incidentally, there is nothing contradictory about 'one anothering' and shepherding; both have a place.

Skills and competencies

I'm not sure that we need to define skills, or need to distinguish skills from gifts. It would be simplistic to say that a skill is different because we can work at it, because we are also called to 'fan into flame the gift of God' (2 Timothy 1:6). Practice does not necessarily make perfect, but practice does make practice a lot easier!

Most people could reach a certain prescribed standard in most identifiable skills, but they may not have the desire. There is an old joke: 'How many psychiatrists does it take to change a light bulb? Seven, but only provided that the light bulb really wants to change!' My father was very capable in the electrical side of DIY, and was very keen to teach me. In my teenage years, I was not very keen to learn, especially at the time from him! To this day, with A-level physics under my belt, wiring a plug is about the threshold of my practical competence. The desire to learn electrical skills simply wasn't there.

The sporting analogy may serve us well again, as in Chapter 3. I guess many people, if they were to attempt a drop-kick on the rugby pitch, would end up horizontal in the mud, with the ball bobbing only a few feet away. At the five-thousandth attempt, the prospects of the ball sailing cleanly between the posts forty yards away are vastly improved. We can isolate the skills in sport, and work at them, but the critical presumption would be that you want to be proficient in drop-kicking.

In business training, there has been a big increase in the emphasis on competencies, and rightly so. We can reduce the difficulties experienced by some people in their jobs to a series of competency shortfalls, define the acceptable standard, and train people to these standards. The competencies can often be acquired by 'on the job' experience, much as we defined coaching in Chapter 3. The whole range of National Vocational Qualification accreditation is based on this philosophy. Even since its inception, there have been improvements, reducing the paperwork and focusing on the relevance of the skill to the job.

There are many aspects of Christian leadership that can be reduced to a set of competencies as well. None of us was born an expert in a particular field; we had to work at it. Delegation, asking questions, conflict resolution, small group dynamics, goal setting, establishing priorities and public communication would be some obvious examples.

The positives and negatives of our motive profile

The next category of weakness involves our personal motivation. I want to suggest that our strengths and weaknesses are often different branches and fruit that actually come from the same roots and origins. All personality tools offer an understanding that includes this dimension. The work of George New and David Cormack (*Why Did I Do That?* pp. 122 ff.), based on the insights of David McClelland, illustrates the positive elements and the 'dark side' quite clearly. McClelland identifies three primary social motives that dominate the bulk of our thinking and activity. Each of us has all three drives, but in different proportions; the mix is firmly established by our mid-teens. Each drive can be well managed and used constructively, but along with these opportunities come predictable vulnerabilities. (See table p. 101.)

The potential for these negative elements to have a major impact will always be present. They come with the person's strengths – you have both sides of the coin or none. We cannot cast the negative potential out or prescribe medication. No training course will prevent the possibility of the dark side emerging. It's no use saying that we want the good side but we wish that did not also bring the down side. The primary responsibility for improvement lies with the individual. They need to recognise and understand the negative potential of the desirable features. Only they can change their mental tapes, and fall into bad practice for shorter periods of time and less frequently. St Paul highlights the difficulty in his own life (Romans 7:17–19).

The solution to some weaknesses lies in a team forum

The work of Meredith Belbin has received wide publicity and acceptance since it was first developed in the 1960s and 70s. His insights demonstrate another dimension of strengths and corresponding weaknesses. The remedy this time is quite different: some apparent deficiencies are best solved by working in a team rather than trying to fulfil all the roles

STRENGTHS AND WEAKNESSES 101

Primary social motive	Typical positive characteristics	Predictable vulnerabilities
Achievement	Diligent	Workaholic
	High standards	Perfectionist
	Likes clear goals	Reluctant delegator
	Acquires technical expertise	Mediocre communication levels
	Enjoys working alone	Does not see the benefits of teamwork
	Likes a challenge	Impatient with the standards of others
Affiliation	Warm and accepting	Reluctant to work alone
	Empathetic	Avoids confrontation
	Good team member	Too many long meetings
	Sensitive to people's needs	Ultra-sensitive
	Supportive	Insufficient task focus
	Maintains a wide network of friends	Needs perpetual affirmation
Power	Training, coaching, developing others	Manipulation, control, domination
	Good manager of others	Low consideration of others' wishes
	Effective influencer	Too concerned for status and image
	Initiates and leads change	May like too much independence
	Natural leadership/ chief executive	Can feel very vulnerable
	Can give immense loyalty	Upset if their value is not recognised

needed in a team by yourself. To illustrate from soccer, it is a pointless comment on an excellent goalkeeper to say that he does not score goals; in the choir, not being a tenor is no criticism of being a good bass. Belbin identified eight roles that are necessary for effective teamwork, which include wise decision-making (written up in Chapter 14 of my book *Leadership Tool Kit*).

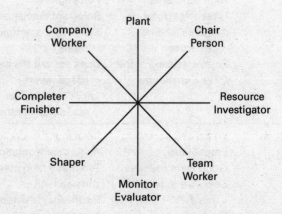

TEAM ROLES

Except for the Plant, the titles are fairly self-explanatory. With eight roles, I cannot resist showing them as the key points of the compass, but the four axes hold some interest and insights. It is not at all unusual to be strong at both ends of the diagonal axes, but it is rare to be good at both contributions on the vertical and horizontal axes. The majority of people who are strong in any of Plant, Monitor Evaluator, Resource Investigator and Completer Finisher would be well-advised to work with another person who can complement them at the other end of that axis.

Let me illustrate. A good friend of mine is a songwriter and worship leader. He is highly creative and thinks on a big scale: if you ask him to bring a guitar to a midweek small group meeting to lead a few songs, he can immediately envisage a choir of a hundred voices and a fifty-piece orchestra. Why settle for less? Needless to say, there aren't enough hours in the

Title of contribution	Function	Positive characteristics	Permissible weaknesses
Plant	Source of original ideas	Creative, unorthodox, imaginative	Impractical, unrealistic
Monitor Evaluator	Accurate judgement	Pragmatic, detached, clear thinking	Cold, clinical, critical, uninspiring
Resource Investigator	Knows the team's context, brings fresh information	Wide outside contacts, extrovert, inquisitive	Does not sustain interest, little task focus
Completer Finisher	Finishes the job, dots 'i's and crosses 't's	Attention to detail, thorough, precise	Low people skills, perfectionist, nit-picking in details
Company Worker	Strategic planning	Practical, diligent, administrative skills, structured thinker	Inflexible, conservative
Team Worker	Oils the wheels, listens and interprets, brings harmony	Relational, sensitive, accepting	Avoids confrontation, indecisive, low emphasis on results
Chair Person	Integrates the individual contributions, holds the process to the agreed agenda	Accepting of diverse contributions, clear sense of purpose and direction	Not necessarily creative or academic
Shaper	Challenges the mediocre and the slow, strives for the best	Dynamic, lots of drive, passionate	Tetchy, irritable, intolerant

day for him to express all his creativity and he has to work with a Monitor Evaluator to assess the practical limits of his musical flair within any project. It would be pointless, and maybe destructive and crippling, to send him on courses about evaluation, practical decision-making and risk assessment; certainly it would inhibit his creativity.

A similar mutual dependence can arise between the Resource Investigator and the Completer Finisher. They are very different animals and sometimes have real difficulty communicating with each other. Look again at the descriptions in the table – they are chalk and cheese. We should not expect anybody to epitomise both roles; nor if they are strong in one feature should we expect them to set about improving in the other. Let another person make that contribution, do it better and enjoy doing it. The usual answer to weaknesses within Belbin's roles is to work interdependently and more as a team.

Knowledge

A lack of knowledge is a problem that has a relatively simple solution: learning and studying. We may also need to make a distinction between knowledge that we must retain and information that we can retrieve quickly. Reading, along with analysis, note-taking and memorising, is a part of the process of assimilation. While many people have a certain capacity for these methods of absorbing information, not everybody chooses them as a preference. It's not just that limited techniques of literacy or slow reading can be the barrier; just as people are not equally motivated to acquire skills, so we don't all want to research and distil pages of text to acquire knowledge. The use of audio tapes can be a useful substitute, partly because reading costs a lot of time and listening to tapes can be combined with other activities such as driving.

My general comment on this section is that learning, studying and the acquisition of knowledge are treated as the correct solution to a weakness far too frequently. I don't think that this mistake is primarily a result of inaccurate diagnosis, but more down to presuppositions about possible solutions. Too often knowledge is seen as the universal panacea. More often the solution lies in finding the wisdom to apply the knowledge appropriately.

Emotional competence

Recently there has been increasing research into the concept of emotional intelligence. The impetus has come from the recognition that some people in managerial positions with a high IQ and a wide range of management competencies are still relatively unsuccessful. It now seems quite possible that one of the missing ingredients towards their success includes a range of factors loosely headed 'emotional intelligence/competence'. The sum of these capabilities will determine an individual's ability to cope with the demands and stresses of their work. Various authors have produced lists and tests, with their own insights into the key ingredients of emotional intelligence. My efforts are a combination:

Intrapersonal competencies
- Self-awareness.
- Coming to an accurate self-image.
- The capacity for personal development.

Interpersonal competencies
- Empathising and sensitivity.
- Influencing.
- The ability to make wise decisions in complex problems around people and personalities.

The ability to manage stress
- Resilience.
- Sustaining behaviour consistent with core values under duress.
- Maintaining motivation and energy.

The ability to manage the emotional responses
- Coping with different states of mind, e.g. fear, disappointment, optimism and happiness.
- Containment of mood swings within acceptable limits.
- The ability to 'bounce back' relatively quickly.

Later on in the book we will consider some ways of improving our emotional competencies. I hope that this consideration of responses to weaknesses has been constructive for you. As a diagnostic tool, it has dug me out of many difficult mentoring situations. However, please don't think that it will solve all the problems you meet when dealing with weaknesses. For some problems there are no solutions – yet! When I was writing this chapter, a minister who is a longstanding friend telephoned me, facing some major decisions. He often turns to me as one of a number of people who could help him; I was not his sole counsellor. After some exploratory discussion, we agreed that the root of his problem was that he is essentially a driven person, to an unhealthy degree. In his teenage years, he was not as successful academically as he would have hoped.

Now the apparent lack of success in any area of his life haunts him. He is showing evidence of the dark side of his achievement drive but is not yet able to face the roots. More time is needed. To everything there is a time, including a time to learn; for him it's not yet.

Mark Twain's often-quoted words might be a good way to end the chapter: 'When I was a boy of 14 my father was so ignorant I could hardly stand to have the old man around. But when I got to be 21, I was astonished at how much he had learned in seven years.' The essential ingredient in mastering our weaknesses is the desire to change our perspectives.

8

Asking Questions

Initially, my work in the Christian sector exclusively involved training in the range of subjects surrounding leadership. The first major shift in emphasis occurred around 1991 when a few organisations asked me to undertake consultancies. The second change, in the mid-90s, brought much more focus on the development of individuals in one-to-one settings, and that role has continued to increase. I sometimes ask myself why this external mentoring has increased. Hopefully a lack of training effectiveness on my courses is not the only reason! One possible explanation is that 'externalness' is seen as bringing greater objectivity and comes without the baggage of internal politics. Motives are presumed to be purer. Another reason might be that as mentors we accrue experience rapidly (a considerable proportion of my life is concerned with people development). The recognition of how questions could dramatically alter my coaching, mentoring and discipling ministries was the single biggest growth event in sixteen years as a consultant to churches. In both of my previous books, I have written extensively about the benefits of questions, without yet being quite convinced that I have fully expressed my heart, or really communicated the power of questions.

The principal key to asking good questions is actually rooted in listening. Without repeating swathes of material on this important subject, pitch your own skills and attitudes against these criteria:

- Do you avoid thinking about your reply before others have finished speaking?
- Do you believe that you can learn something worthwhile from all the people you meet?
- Do you try to hear the heart of what is being said?
- Do you continue to listen beyond the point where you are really interested?
- Do you consistently take into account the personality of the speaker as you attribute meaning to the speaker's words?
- How frequently do you interrupt the speaker?
- How often do you rephrase and reflect to check your understanding?

Our own paradigms greatly affect our listening. We absorb even the fine detail of comments that reinforce our mindsets, but are inclined to filter information contrary to our own viewpoint. Listening is often hard work, but that's the price of asking the right questions.

Jesus the questioner

As we regard Jesus as our model in all things, then he must be the supreme questioner. Indeed this is the case, for in the four gospels, depending on the versions and translations used, he poses some 316 questions, plus another in Acts 9:4 and 22:7, 'Saul, Saul, why do you persecute me?' Taking out the obvious duplicates, we have a total of 233. If we further remove the questions he includes in the stories he tells, such as 'Didn't you agree to work for a denarius?' (Matthew 20:13) and 'How much do you owe my master?' (Luke 16:5), we are left with a round 200. These are the real questions he puts to the crowds, his disciples, to individuals and to his opponents, and they fall into various categories according to their purpose.

Some are rhetorical and are not really seeking an answer but are used as a teaching point or to confirm an obvious truth, such as 'Do you bring in a lamp to put it under a bowl?' (Mark 4:21), and 'Which of you, if his son asks for bread, will give him a stone?' (Matthew 7:9). Another category is the tough questions he sometimes puts to his disciples and friends: 'Who do you say I am?' (Matthew 16:15) and 'Do you still not see or understand? Are your hearts hardened?' (Mark 8:17). Finally, there are the questions with which he puts his opponents and enemies on the spot: 'John's baptism . . . Was it from heaven, or from men?' (Matthew 21:25), 'What is written in the Law? How do you read it?' (Luke 10:26), 'Which is lawful on the Sabbath: to do good or to do evil, to save life or to kill?' (Mark 3:4) and 'Can any of you prove me guilty of sin?' (John 8:46).

As is the way with much Hebraic discussion, he would often answer a question with another, as he did to the rich young ruler: 'Why do you call me good?' (Mark 10:18). Sometimes the question was to elicit a specific short-term response, as to the blind Bartimaeus: 'What do you want me to do for you?' (Mark 10:51); and sometimes to counter criticism: 'Haven't you read what David did when he and his companions were hungry?' (Matthew 12:3). Once he asked a question in utter despair: 'My God, my God, why have you forsaken me?' (Matthew 27:46). Whatever the situation, there was always a specific purpose to the question; it was never a random way of continuing the conversation. This is a key hallmark of the good questioner.

As to the type of Jesus' questions, there are ninety-five that require only a 'yes/no' answer and these are either of the pretty obvious rhetorical sort, or are designed to pin down his pro-tagonist to a commitment one way or the other. There are thirty of the factual 'When? Where? Who? How many? How long?' questions, and forty-five of the 'What? How? Which?' questions. The largest single category, of which there are thirty, is the 'Why?' question, which is always intended to be the most revealing.

We should not be surprised at Jesus' mastery of the ques-tion technique. Remember that in Genesis 3 we are given the basics of good and bad questioning. The serpent says: 'Did God really say, "You must not eat from any tree in the garden"?' – a loaded question which contains a misquotation and yet demands only a narrow 'yes/no' answer. Contrast that with God's three questions: 'Where are you?', 'Who told you that you were naked?' and 'What is this you have done?' (NIV) Pertinent to the context and demanding of a thoughtful per-sonal response, this is the pattern of questioning that Jesus used and which can help us in our own daily enquiry. (I am greatly indebted to Robert McLeish, a true friend and former training colleague, for this research into the questions of Jesus. Robert was previously Head of Corporate Manage-ment Training at the BBC. He had a significant impact in my development; his skills and generous nature have served many people well.)

As I have prepared this book, I've read widely around the

subject of communication, probably trying to add credibility to my own experience! Many authors have included substantial lists of 'good and useful' questions to start a mentoring meeting. While I will also give you some suggestions later, we are all in danger of missing a key point. Who decides the criteria for this 'good' quality? If we are truly trying to serve the disciple, the real grading of our questions is in their hands. We might think that questions around issues such as calling, character and family are important, but the disciple might be doing brilliantly in those areas and has come to us with a problem that we would never have guessed or predicted. Partly for this reason, the single question that has served me best at the start of a meeting or process is: 'Where are you itching?' It might sound very colloquial, but the words recognise that there is no point in me scratching where the disciple isn't itching! In some meetings when we have been under time pressure, we have also got to the root of the problem very quickly via this question.

There are various possible outcomes to asking questions. If your goal is to be a facilitative sounding board, the quality and sequence of the questions is critical. If you want to reach something closer to a dialogue rather than the Spanish Inquisition, then again the questions at the early stages determine your prospects. But apart from the single question above, it's probably best to focus on areas for discussion rather than specific examples. I can't train you far beyond the initial question anyway. Questioning is a bit like tennis: we can concentrate on the service, but we cannot plan the third shot of the rally until we have seen the return of the service, although there are a few predictable combinations. There are far too many variants within the possible replies to your first question for us to plan the next question.

Areas for discussion

Questions directed at these six subject areas have usually yielded important results:

- vision
- barriers and blocks
- commitment to the first steps
- the costs
- repeat scenarios
- the emotional life

Vision

Helping people to identify and clarify their vision, and to reach it, is at the very heart of mentoring. The time span that we can look ahead to is certainly a variable – vision may stretch anything from three to ten years ahead. I have written about the process of building vision elsewhere (in *Small Group Know How*), but suffice to say for now that it will be necessary for an individual to visit the issues of values and life purpose as preliminary steps. Eventually, however, vision must contain the concept of destination and might be accessed by any of these questions:

- What do you expect to be celebrating X years from now?
- What will you be thanking God for?
- What will you have become?
- What will you be doing?
- What will you have caused?
- What will be your major impact?

Many people find it very hard even to consider the concepts associated with vision. You may well get initial answers like 'Whatever God wills!' Don't worry about that response: vision-building takes time and seldom comes in one go. Ask them to identify at least some components of what they want, even if they cannot see the full picture.

The benefits of the two questions 'What do you believe God is saying?' and 'What do you want?' also prove quite interesting. Sometimes the first option really touches people, but the second is assumed to be selfish and raises hackles. Some folk still assume that the answers to the two questions must be different, and that God's main hobby is thwarting the desires he has put into our hearts! The replies tell me a great deal about the disciple's theology of guidance. It's important to encourage them to own their heart's desire.

Frequently values and vision come into their own when we are looking for answers to choices. A few years ago, three people I respect and who I know care about me gave me very different advice. One suggested that I adapt my first book for the secular market, another thought that I should improve my master's degree to a doctorate, and the third thought that I should write a second Christian book. Well, they could not all be correct simultaneously, purely because I also had to earn my crust! But at any crossroads, if we know the destination it will be clear which way we should turn. I still feel called to spend the bulk but not all of my time in the Christian sector, so I did not write a secular book. I have every opportunity to continue my studies without undertaking additional formal qualifications. The vision answered my questions and I duly carried on writing Christian books.

Barriers and blocks

Having talked about some elements of a desired destination, the next area for discussion should involve the possible obstacles. Some of these questions might be useful:

- What could get in the way?
- What might prove to be the biggest sticking point?
- Which people could be the centre of opposition?
- What skill shortages could limit your progress?
- Why do you think that the timing is appropriate now?
- Is your passion for this vision sufficient to carry you over these hurdles?

The barriers identified at this stage can be grouped into two sub-sections. The potential blockages are viewed as either internal or external to the disciple. Internal issues include skills, time availability and emotional resilience, whereas external factors cover circumstances, the weather, the family, finances, the elders and other people. We need to ask at least two questions to help them think through the source and impact of these blockages. So probe questions like 'Which of these factors are within your own control?' and 'What can you do about them?' are important. The answers are not objective; it's their chosen standpoint that we are exploring, because that is reality for them. If the disciple thinks that virtually all the barriers are outside their control, that supposition needs challenging.

Commitment to the first steps

At the end of every mentoring session, ask the disciple to summarise the action steps that have been agreed. At least some of the often conceptual thinking must be closed down into measurable goals. Even the greatest visions on earth had to start with a single step and these steps are sometimes quite surprising. For the Israelites, the taking of the Promised Land started with killing lambs and daubing some blood on the doors whilst Moses performed some amazing miracles with his walking staff in front of Pharaoh!

The questions that we need to ask at this stage include:

- What steps will you have taken by the next time we meet?
- What will you need to do first?
- What else could you begin simultaneously with that step?
- Whose help will you need to enlist?
- What information will you need before you make a decision?
- What help do you need to overcome the initial blockages?

The costs

Every change has a cost attached. The costs may be emotional or financial and very often also have a time component. Things like gaining an extra qualification might affect family time, pursuing a hobby might cause guilt feelings about work, pushing a skill beyond the present threshold might cost nervous energy, and a new job may involve the family moving house. We always have to live with the minuses of an option that we choose, and, assuming that we cannot have cake and eat it, we often have to forsake the pluses of the options we eliminate. We should always encourage people to count the costs at the outset, in so far as those costs can be predicted.

Repeat scenarios

Part of the mentoring process requires us to encourage people to learn from their experiences. I've found that people have appreciated these two sequences:

1. What's gone well recently? What was so good about it? How did you feel about it? If you come to similar situations in the future, what would you have to do to *ensure* another success? What encouragement have you taken?

2. What's not gone too well recently? What went wrong? What would you have to do differently to really increase the chances of success? What have you learnt?

The emotional life

These questions usually offer the disciple the chance to explore deeper issues. The possible danger is that the conversation stays focused on the past. The subject matter might appear more like counselling, but good counsellors still want the ultimate outcome to be future-focused. Some of these questions might serve you well, but don't use too many of them at once!

- What drains you emotionally?
- What builds you up?
- What have been the most significant events in your life?
- What experiences have been the most traumatic?
- How have people affirmed you? What have they said about you?
- How do you relax?
- How are you sleeping?
- Who are your closest friends? What do you enjoy about them?

- What internal conflicts are there in your life?
- Who has influenced you over the last few months?
- How are you balancing the family, work, church and personal time?
- What are you reading this week?
- What values are driving the use of your finances?

Extension questions

In mentoring, there will be times when we need to encourage the disciple to think deeply about their behaviour and the premisses that drive it. Never make assumptions about motives – we can *observe* behaviour but we can only *explore* the reasons behind it. Here are a group of questions that you can use if you feel that the conversation is stubbornly superficial:

- How do you know?
- What would be the counter-arguments?
- Why are you so certain?
- What alternative courses of action have you ruled out?
- What might be the unintended consequences?
- How would you turn that idea into action?
- How else could you achieve the same end product?

Monitoring questions

It's important to be able to review goals and progress, and I mean have a review, not just a post-mortem! We need to evaluate the results during the allocated time period and not only at the end, when the consequences of failure might be severe. So questions along these lines may help:

- How will you measure progress?
- What will be the initial signs that you are on the right path?
- Does this major goal need any smaller, subordinate goals? What might they be?
- What will be the first landmark on the way?

Ten keys to asking good questions

1. Initially you might ask the right questions in a rather abrupt manner. Don't worry – persevere. Soon you will be asking the right questions in a relaxed way. Questioning is a skill, so it needs practice.
2. The real key to asking the right question is dedicated listening.
3. The disciple determines the benefit of the question, not the mentor.
4. There are alternative outcomes to asking questions. At the extremes, you might end up as a sounding board or with a more 'equal' dialogue.
5. There is a place for the closed question (i.e. requiring the 'Yes' or 'No' answer) but 'How?' and 'Why?' are likely to start the most productive questions.
6. Be prepared to challenge inconsistencies and shallow responses.
7. Be aware that the smallest changes in words or intonation are important as the disciple attributes meaning to your question.
8. We usually close down real exploration too early. Ask questions that push for further creative options before coming to a conclusion.
9. Every session should contain something about vision, blocks, first steps or costs.

10. Questions are the very essence of the non-directive approach to discipling.

An exercise I have used frequently during seminars on coaching and mentoring (and you might like to try it at a social event or in other casual conversations) is to get people into pairs to discover how many questions they need to ask before they cause the other person either to stop and think or to acknowledge that the question has been useful to them.

9
Feedback

Whatever type of developmental relationship you consider and forge, feedback will be an integral part from time to time. Even in the most non-directive roles, there will be occasions when the mentor or spiritual director will have to make their views known. In a coaching relationship particularly, performance-related feedback is central to the disciple's development. I am going to take a broad view of the concept of feedback, because many of the principles and skills are identical in all the applications of feedback. The content might be positive or negative; we might be commenting on a skill, an attitude or a particular behaviour. We may be translating feedback as encouragement, exhortation, correction or affirmation. They all have their place, and following the ideas of this chapter, they can all hopefully be done better.

There are many scriptures that illustrate some of the different aspects of giving and receiving feedback. Quite a few of the verses containing the phrase 'one another' revolve around the possible applications of feedback. Here is a range, taken primarily from the New Testament:

'She has done a beautiful thing to me.' (Matthew 26:10)

Let the word of Christ dwell in you richly as you teach and admonish one another with all wisdom, and as you sing psalms, hymns and spiritual songs with gratitude in your hearts to God. (Colossians 3:16)

Now we ask you, brothers, to respect those who work hard among you, who are over you in the Lord and who admonish you. (1 Thessalonians 5:12)

Whoever loves discipline loves knowledge, but he who hates correction is stupid. (Proverbs 12:1)

All Scripture is God-breathed and is useful for teaching, rebuking, correcting and training in righteousness, so that the man of God may be thoroughly equipped for every good work. (2 Timothy 3:16–17)

The reference from Colossians recommends that we yearn for 'all wisdom' as we admonish, and the Proverbs verse is pretty outspoken! Feedback is common throughout Scripture. We need to look at how to use it better today.

National and church cultures

Straight speaking is appreciated to different degrees in different national cultures. Among the Europeans, the Swedes and the Dutch have something of a reputation for saying things as they are, rather than wrapping them up or holding back. The stereotypical brashness of the USA, however, might be an over-statement. I have found them relatively free in giving positive feedback, but much more reluctant to criticise. Perhaps oddly, given some of the roots of quality management, the Japanese are especially cautious about anything that could be construed as causing anyone to lose face.

While there has been a substantial emphasis on assertiveness in the UK over recent years, I think that traditionally we are as reluctant as most nations to give feedback, particularly with a negative slant. It is common to all humankind that we want to be liked and appreciated, so we will naturally shy away from behaviour that experience has proved threatening to our relationships. John Harvey-Jones puts it this way:

> Frankness is not an admired characteristic among British people, and in some cases is actually considered to be slightly uncouth. Truthfulness and openness are particularly difficult aims to have in a British organisation where so much of our education and background have been devoted to concealing our feelings and to suffer heroically without protest. (Quoted in Larry Reynolds, *The Trust Effect*, p.153)

For some time in business circles, the old-fashioned word 'candour' became popular; it summarised the open type of climate that companies were striving for. Each church has its own peculiar culture, like any other organisation. Probably the average culture of UK churches compounds the negative impact of the national flavour. The behaviour in most churches seems to be based on phrases like 'gentle Jesus, meek and mild' and 'turn the other cheek', and issues are swept under the carpet. It's a very strange myth for Christians to perpetuate, given that the gospels dispel the idea that Jesus modelled such a passive approach. In studies about organisations, it has been shown that it is especially difficult to forge the right climate where there is excessive bureaucracy and a strong sense of hierarchy; where the sexes are treated as unequal, or if social background and education are key differentiators. Our churches need to avoid these features if we want to create the best climate for discipling.

Seeking feedback

We should be trying to foster a climate where learners clamour for information – it's much better than when the emphasis is on the coach. The first and obvious benefit is that most of the information we impart will be seen as relevant by the disciple. If the coach/mentor can limit the width of their answers, the content will remain focused on areas the disciple really wants to explore. Secondly, the whole problem of the timing of the feedback, which we will look at soon, is dissolved. The coach is not left treading on eggshells, wondering when might be the appropriate moment.

We need to teach people how to ask for, and listen to, feedback. So we must encourage them to ask the right questions. A budding preacher, after one of their earliest sermons, might ask: 'Was that OK this morning?' That sort of phraseology can create a slight quandary. Are they just looking for plaudits or acceptance? How much detail do they want? A better sort of question would narrow the scope of the discussion. 'What percentage of the congregation do you think were really engaged?' 'Were there enough stories and illustrations today?' The learner has a big role to play in generating the best sort of feedback. Their contribution can make it much easier for the coach to deliver messages palatably.

Receiving and interpreting feedback

It's important that we can handle criticism if we want to be able to give it from time to time! And apart from other possible reasons, we need to model the right attitudes that enable us to receive feedback and integrate the lessons into the learning process. Too often relationships seem to be at risk because conflict is too frequently the outcome. Here are some of the important steps to receiving feedback well.

1. We need to listen carefully. The key is to keep an open mind. There's likely to be a measure of truth in the content, even if we could sometimes take exception to elements of the style. We should try and imagine the speaker's feelings about the behaviour they are describing to us.

2. We need to look for patterns in what people are saying when they give us feedback. If there is a great deal of common ground in what we are being told, it is more likely that their perceptions are accurate. Most of us are unlikely to make radical changes on the basis of isolated comments, but we should treat feedback as a hypothesis to be tested further. If we sense that the feedback we are receiving generally has some substance to it, then we can ask questions that seek further information about those manifestations.

3. Some sort of primitive cost/benefit analysis about the changes we could make is useful. We should be looking to implement things with a minimal cost that bring considerable advantages. I worked with one leader in this way, to the great satisfaction of all parties. He is quite brilliant but easily misunderstood and seemed by nature to be detached and aloof. Actually, he is very caring, but that's not the first impression. He virtually never showed that he was paying attention, yet over a sustained period he proved to have a remarkable retention rate

for detail from previous conversations. All that was required to change people's perceptions were a few communicative grunts and some eye contact. He's proved to be a quick learner too.

4. We can improve our response to praise because it's often handled at least as badly as criticism! It can certainly leave us suspicious or embarrassed. Sometimes we devalue it with comments like: 'I guess I was just lucky today'; 'It wasn't me; it was the Lord who did it'; 'In my shoes you would have done exactly the same thing yourself'; 'It was nothing really'. It's possible to switch off because we are so sure there will be a 'but' statement soon, or, working on the reciprocity principle, we think that we must find something similarly effusive to say about the other person. Sometimes we assume that it's just ingratiating flattery. The best way of receiving praise is to thank the person, and then to ask a probe question: 'What particularly helped you?'; 'What might be the first steps in applying the material?'

Giving feedback

(a) The amount

I believe that the quotation 'See everything; overlook a great deal; correct a little' is attributed to Pope John XXIII. It's a good basis for us to work on. The quantity of feedback we want to give is probably determined by the amount of change we want to see. The greater danger is that we expect too much change rather than too little, either through impatience or over-optimism. So it's better to say too little rather than too much, provided we are capable of focusing on the key issues.

Nevertheless, people learn best in different ways. The research about learning initially carried out by David Kolb and developed by Peter Honey and Alan Mumford has become

popular. He talks about four learning styles: the activist, the
reflector, the theorist and the pragmatist. (They are written up,
with a questionnaire and norms, in chapter 6 of one of my previous books, *Leadership Tool Kit*.) In an ideal world, a rounded
approach to learning integrating all four styles produces the
best results, but there is no doubt that we all have preferences.
People who strongly favour the theorist approach need much
more detail in their feedback sessions. They learn best when
they understand *why* things work. Activists and pragmatists
just want to go and apply the lessons immediately. The reflector will happily go away and read a book.

Just consider for a moment the scenario of a church with
no feedback. Some random learning would still take place, but
without members being able to easily capitalise on the experience gained by other people. Perhaps a bigger danger would
be that everyone else receives the comments, rather than the
learner. By being reluctant to give and accept feedback, we
provoke gossip.

(b) The timing

There are two good reasons for giving feedback as close to the
event or behaviour as possible. First, this practice minimises
the danger of repeated mistakes and avoids the possibility of
setting a pattern that takes some breaking. The longer
anybody spends typing with two fingers, the harder it is to
learn the proper technique. (Or, in my case, I now deem it
impossible!) Second, continuing the insights of Kolb's work,
the activists need their feedback especially close to the event.
Life for them is about rich and varied experiences, approaching opportunities without prejudice, and often repeating their
mistakes. Feedback must be close to the event for them to
recall the feelings and the stages that proved crucial. If you

start a feedback session with reflective language like 'Can you remember doing this? It was about eight months ago' the honest answer will be 'no'. If their sermons are going to improve, you need to catch them coming down the pulpit steps, and no later!

There is a counter-demand though: feedback should be given at the best time emotionally for the learner. Formal sessions have an advantage in this respect in that the disciple will be expecting such comments. We are unlikely to get a positive response if they are off guard, emotionally disorientated, feeling vulnerable after just exerting themselves in the action under scrutiny, about to go to an important meeting, or engrossed in a task that they see as demanding.

The final benefit of delaying feedback is that we should not assume that one mistake is a generalisation. For example, if somebody appears to lose their temper on one occasion, the context may include extreme provocation, a great deal of history of bad feeling between the parties and a combination of other stress factors. Whilst the label of sin should not be diluted, one incident in itself does not constitute a major character defect.

(c) The style

Before setting out to give feedback, first consider whether a question might serve you better. The most obvious use of feedback is as a coach, commenting on a technical skill in which you are very proficient and at home. In most other situations, the views of the disciple are at least as important. Initially, it is usually better to ask for their comments and feelings rather than trying to impose a solution.

I find the following anonymous quotation very powerful.

Diplomacy is to truth and falsehood what grey is to black and white. Use your diplomacy palette wisely. Call something grey when it's clearly black and white and you're down. Call it greyish when it's greyish and you're OK. Don't lose your ability to paint in pure black or white by contaminating each with the other. If you must be diplomatic, know you are being so.

In other words, try honesty as a first, not a last, resort. It is a false assumption that mincing words will sustain trust and relationship, but it's also worth remembering that honesty does not have to be brutal.

Look at five similar but very different statements of feedback:

- 'You were twenty minutes late for the team meeting.'
- 'Your time management skills are poor.'
- 'You have a poor attitude to the team.'
- 'You are a poor timekeeper.'
- 'You don't respect people.'

These statements are respective comments on:

- a behaviour in one particular incident
- a set of skills
- an attitude
- an integral part of their personality
- a core value

We should use the first type of comment by far the most frequently; focus on the behaviour. It has the best prospects of a good reception. Repeated lateness may indicate an attitude problem, but we cannot be sure initially. Remember, we can *observe* behaviour, but we can only *explore* the reasons for it. An additional benefit of the first type is that it is the easiest to put right; it's simple to choose to be punctual at the next meeting, but much harder to develop skills or cultivate a different attitude. Let's be tough on behaviour but soft towards people.

Finally for this section, a few quick hints on the style issues of feedback. Focus on the future, not the past. Feedback is designed to cause an improvement, not just a discussion. Highlight the consequences of the behaviour that you have observed. And don't try too hard. If the message isn't accepted, be prepared to back off. You are unlikely to win the argument and guaranteed to damage the relationship.

(d) The positive alternative

As we have already said, honesty is the best policy. That principle supersedes the design of artificial numerical boundaries between positive and negative statements. I have often heard comments suggesting that we should give three lots of praise and encouragement for every critical statement. Other people swear by the sandwich principle – put the critical filling between two thick slices of praise – reckoning that it's important to start and end on a positive note. Being supportive does not mean constantly praising; we don't want to produce false self-perceptions.

The real solution to the balance of positives and negatives is that we integrate criticism and the offer of a positive alternative on every feedback occasion. Instead of just saying, 'This is not very good,' we need to say, 'Here is how it can be done better and here are the benefits.' Paul regularly employs this style in his letters to the New Testament churches. Colossians 3:1–17 is a good example – the full passage is worth reading, not just the single verse that I quoted at the beginning of this chapter. Ephesians 4:17–22 also illustrates the principle very well – many individual verses contain the full contrast between unrighteous behaviour and wholesome activity.

(e) Motives

I'm not going to encourage you to wait until your motives are 100 per cent pure before you give any further feedback, or we would all be waiting a very long time! Yet we should examine ourselves regularly, especially if the path of discipling has been a little rocky recently. Any components of point scoring, manipulation, flattery or revenge will hinder the disciple's desire to hear what we have to say.

(f) Trust

I feel that this chapter could be significant in enhancing the quality of discipling within any church. Too often feedback has produced stormy discussions, if my experience is remotely like yours. The bottom line goes back to Chapter 6: it's trust. Good feedback can improve relationships, but any feedback, formal or informal, takes place within the parameters of the existing relationship. If the friendship is solid and proven, the climate will be positive. You could get away with all sorts of blunders because the disciple knows that your heart is for them. On the other hand, if the relationship is wobbly, you could do everything by the book with very little prospect of success.

Finally, here is a table to illustrate the differences between feedback and criticism. I want to leave you with positive recollections in a memorable format!

Feedback should be:

Actionable	Advice should be practical, realistic and something that can be used.
Blame free	Tough on issues, not on people.
Calm	Generally the manner should be cool, not full of emotion.
Dispassionate	Factual and objective.
Enlightening	Don't tell people what they already know!
Future-oriented	Focus on the future, not the past, to produce change.
Generous	Mix positive and negative feedback; keep to a narrow negative agenda.

10

Down in the Valleys

Despite our best efforts, we all experience some periods in our lives when we are spiritually low. God seems very remote and unwilling to answer our prayers, the word is arid and feels inaccessible, and bouncy Christians are a pain in the neck! These are the seasons in the valley as opposed to those on the mountain-top. There are times when God uses them mightily, but more frequently there is very little learning either during the lean spell or after the event. Sometimes these flat periods are profoundly debilitating, and so I would like to spend a chapter exploring strategies for handling them better. We all want to experience fewer dips in our Christian walk, and would like each dip to be less prolonged and less deep than previously. I try to teach on the things where I've made some progress myself and I think in forty years as a Christian I can honestly say that one of my strengths is that I'm fairly consistent. That level might be consistently lower than you experience, but my peaks and troughs are not a long way apart.

I'm addressing this issue of the valley seasons for a variety of reasons. First, our walk is for the glory of God. Jesus is utterly consistent, and as the ultimate goal of discipleship is to be more like him, our goal in discipling should be to work towards that standard also. Second, we have personal responsibilities towards the corporate body of Christ. We could parallel the body to a coal fire. If we want to burn brightly, every coal needs to be glowing. Every damp coal that fails to contribute positively saps heat from the others; if there are too few burning, the whole fire tends to go out. The New Testament is quite clear that if one member hurts, the whole body hurts. Members also find it very disconcerting when they experience extreme responses from friends. Which mood will they come in today? Are they going to be on a real high and absolutely flying, or will they be down in the dumps? The high seasons are a tremendous blessing to other people; the low times are quite draining all round.

During my time as a Christian, and in some cases within my present church, I have really hurt when people I would classify as true and close friends have known sustained periods down in the ashpit, as Job would say. Two men are leaders of real stature, and their independent valley experiences lasted about a year each. Eventually, they sank to a level where they had forgotten why they went down there at all, and certainly they had forgotten how to get out again. Seeing friends reach this level, and being able to do little to help, was quite harrowing.

Third, if it's disconcerting for the body of Christ when we are inconsistent, then how much more so for the outside world. Part of effective evangelism, I think, must be that if someone wants to talk about real life issues, they have a right to expect a certain consistent response from professing believers. People won't come to us if our quality of life is a poor advertisement for the gospel. Neither will they approach us if our response can vary dramatically from one day to the next. Answers to their questions must be modelled in consistent lives.

This book is primarily about discipling. Dealing with the valley seasons all too frequently seems to become a personal issue between the disciple and God, what we have called 'discipleship'. Nevertheless, I want to include this chapter because the cost of these seasons is often so expensive, and involves not only the individual disciple, but many other people. I also suspect that the cost is sometimes unnecessarily high, beyond any learning benefits. Sadly, I haven't found the keys of success as a discipler in helping folk who are in the valley; sustained, non-judgemental friendship is the best that I have offered.

There are vast theological issues about valleys that I don't feel qualified to unpack fully. My state is consistent: I am a sinner saved by grace. I'm not called to live at a standard that is driven by the expectations of other people; my daily responsibility is to appropriate that grace. Perhaps this challenge is at the centre of the daily Christian walk, whatever my circumstances. I also want to avoid the trap of blame. The standard evangelical answer is all too often 'Pull your socks up and try harder', with the implication 'It's all your own fault'. My understanding of the 'dark night of the soul' theology is minimal, so I have not focused on any possible 'benefits' of the valley experience, but I do know that God's ways and thoughts are much higher than mine (Isaiah 55:8–9).

The temptations of Jesus

Please read Matthew 3:13–4:11. I think it's significant that the temptations of Jesus immediately follow on from the water baptism at the end of chapter 3. This chapter break is artificial and we shouldn't think of it as a break in the text. So the last verse of chapter 3, which must have been a memorable moment, is immediately followed by the temptations: 'And a voice from heaven said, "This is my Son, whom I love; with him I am well pleased." Then Jesus was led by the Spirit into the desert to be tempted by the devil.'

This verse at his water baptism was primarily an affirmation of his sonship. Virtually immediately after this, the first two temptations both start off with the phrase 'If you are the Son of God . . .'. The core temptation, essentially, was to break his relationship with the Father. We are prone to the same temptation, to try to prove ourselves. The work of the enemy is still the same as well: if he can break our communication with God, he has won the skirmish. The longer the rapport remains broken, the better the enemy will be pleased. The only other time that we read about Jesus being tempted is in the Garden of Gethsemane (Matthew 26:39, 42, 44). The prayer makes clear that Jesus would have preferred another path; the temptation was to fail to do the Father's will. Again that is essentially the choice we face each day: doing God's will or choosing our own way.

I think it's significant that when we consider the two main passages about the temptations of Jesus, we see that they are right at the outset of his ministry and right at the end. However, I'm not quite sure what the significance is! Perhaps those points were the defining boundaries in some way. It's sometimes easy for us to say that he was perfect man as well as being perfect God, but equally easy to forget that he experienced all the difficulties and all the temptations that we've felt as humans. That means he probably looked at the opposite sex and was tempted, and I suppose that he looked at the first-century Jewish equivalent of jam doughnuts and was tempted! I believe he experienced, in essence, all the temptations that we face today, but we know that he did not yield. Falling to temptation is often part of the process of drifting down into the valley experience. Let's move on to some practical tips for dealing with these dark times.

1. Use the mountain-top seasons well

We need to use the mountain-top seasons wisely. The times when we are down in the valley are not ideal times for building good strategies for getting out of them. When things are going well, that's the time to build our resources for the tougher seasons in the valley bottom that might lie ahead. Vision, for example, is critical for survival, based on an accurate understanding of the gifts put into our stewardship. When I was first introduced to the powerful concept of vision, I was at a relatively low ebb and it was a few years before I had a picture that raised my game and really excited me.

So what should happen on the mountain-top? We need to understand and enjoy the acceptance of God, both directly from God and via the body of Christ. We need to get into the word of God and polish up on the basic Christian disciplines. The core disciplines are Bible study, prayer and worship. If we don't work on these basic drills when things are going well, then they'll certainly creak when things are going badly.

Recently I was working with a major mission society that focuses on Africa and met again a valued friend I had not seen for some considerable time. Ten years previously he had been in hospital for a prolonged period with a leg seriously damaged in a road accident. For months he could barely walk. Doctors doubted that he would ever walk properly again, let alone have enough muscle to control aeroplane pedals. Simultaneously, his wife was at home in a hospital in the States; she'd had an operation and caught a serious infection that proved to be life-threatening. They were thousands of miles apart and potentially both could have fallen very low spiritually. He remained certain that God had called him to fly aeroplanes. When I met him ten years later, I heard that the leg had healed sufficiently for him to be back flying an aeroplane again. He had hung on to what God had given him to do and trusted that God would remain faithful to his promises. We can't necessarily always interpret the words we have been given; often they are for confirmation rather than as a route map for our lives. We must make sure that they balance up with Scripture. Nevertheless, promises like these can be a great comfort when we are in the valley.

2. Recognise when you are slipping

We need to be very honest with ourselves and recognise the earliest signs of wending our way down into the spiritual darkness. I entitle that understanding 'name it and shame it'. Short term, it's sometimes easier to deny the situation and come up with the standard reply 'No, I'm fine, really' when friends politely enquire about our spiritual wellbeing. It's important to take action at the earliest possible opportunity. I can remember a parallel idea as a student at university. At the beginning of term, not only was there a full attendance at the first lecture of the day, but additionally everybody was down for breakfast, bright-eyed and bushy-tailed. Near the end of term, it was considered a feat if a student had conquered the alarm clock just to get to the lecture on time. Standards had slowly, but steadily, fallen. New norms were understood. If the same thing happens in our Christian life, we are very vulnerable. We can easily forget our former state and aspirations. One definition of backsliding is 'There once was a day when I was closer to God than I am now'. If we can ever say that, then there is some urgency to take action.

3. Be prepared to receive from the body of Christ

Men especially, it is mooted, can find it very challenging to accept help and admit vulnerability. The stiff upper lip mentality is a serious denial of how we were made spiritually and our need for interdependence. I'm not saying that every time we feel a little off colour (again, I mean spiritually) we should put the news in the church notices and tell the whole world. But we might as well be honest about things, because our condition is usually pretty obvious to at least some other people. Sometimes the revelation of our struggle has to come to us from other people, because we are prepared, at least short term, to deny the problem. Good friends don't fall off their chair when we share our difficulties with them. We especially need that sort of friend around us at the difficult times.

In stress management materials – and not only those from a Christian perspective – there are some consistent recommendations: we need the support of other people, especially in the valley seasons, which are particularly stressful. They can offer creative solutions, act as sounding boards, help us with the benefit of their similar experiences, or maybe just listen.

In December 2000, for roughly a week, I had the worst doubts I have ever had in my Christian life. They were horrendous. With hindsight, it's easy to see the combination of circumstances stacked against me. The autumn is always the most intense time of ministry for me; September to November are my busiest months of the year. Additionally, I was working to a deadline on my second book. Life consisted of travelling and ministry, and coming back home to switch on the computer and carry on working. If there was any time left for anything else, I would fall asleep in front of a football game on TV. I lost my reference points entirely – they just weren't there. There seemed to be very little time for informal interaction with my wife or friends.

I had to take action, and the response was to use truth and, to some extent, experience. I've heard imprisoned people quoted as saying, 'If you were in isolation for a long period of time, could you sustain your faith?' That's not a test that I would relish. I recognise that I need contact with normal people, within my church and with others in the neighbourhood. I've now built some strategies to prevent any recurrence of the problem impacting so hard. A key change involves my own church; if I'm away from basic church life for too long, I'm vulnerable. The Sunday meeting is particularly important to me; that's my staple food. When I am asked to undertake weekends of ministry away, people often say, 'We'd like you to do Friday night and Saturday with the leaders. Why not stay and preach on Sunday?' Increasingly now my answer is, 'Thanks, but no. I recognise and accept God's gifts that enable me to conduct the bulk of the weekend, but I need to be at home for a minimum of two Sundays per month, and you've got plenty of people who can preach.'

4. Use truth to repel doubts

A friend of mine, a curate who was leading the church youth group when I was a teenager, told me about his difficult times when he was studying at theological college. Certainly he was at one of the 'better' institutions, but theological courses are renowned for giving you trials (sometimes deliberately and beneficially) as well as more obviously building your faith. He had a pretty serious spiritual nosedive in the middle of his student days. Ultimately, his wife said to him, 'Fine, if it's got that far, why not go the whole hog and just deny your faith, deny Jesus and forget the whole lot!' He couldn't go that far and take the ultimate step. 'In that case,' she said, 'everything else follows because he is who he is. There's no halfway house.' The word of God and his promises are the best antidotes to our wayward feelings.

5. Look for a daily testimony

From time to time, unbelievers say to me challengingly, 'Well, tell me what this Jesus has done for you then. How do you know that he exists?' I don't want to have to resort to an event of many years ago for an answer. The Christian life has got to have more obvious relevance than that. So last year, at New Year, I asked God for a daily testimony, some sort of evidence of his presence every day. I'd like to share one simple example with you that happened in late January.

It was 11.10 on Friday night and a severe problem occurred on the computer. I don't have a wonderful relationship with these machines; in fact it would be fairer to say that I've got a mental blockage with them, dating back to my earliest days of programming in the 60s. If you made a mistake in those days, then you lost everything, the whole program. I felt God say, 'Ask John.' Now John is our neighbour, a very quiet guy, loves computing, and we're beginning to build a friendship. His family home faces our house across the road and he works shifts. It would be very difficult to know whether he was at home or not, asleep or awake; neither would I want to risk disturbing his family at that hour. Instead I tried to telephone my brother, who is also an expert with computers, but, as I remembered later, he and his family had gone away for the weekend. Again God said, 'Ask John.' Reluctantly, I opened the front door – just as John was drawing up in his car! He said, 'I've just been to look at someone's computer. Have you got a problem as well? Let's have a look at it.' The really funny thing is that if I had obeyed God the first time, John wouldn't have been arriving outside; he'd still have been a couple of miles away. Not only was the guidance right, the timing was perfect. (Postscript: experts solve problems in only a few minutes!)

I wish I could say that there has been such evidence and guidance every day. But I *can* say that my testimony is more up to date than in any previous year. It especially came home to me when I received comments on this book from a proof-reader. I had been preparing the material for over a year. Suddenly I realised that God *had* answered my prayer; all my experiences, every day, every moment, are incontrovertible evidence of his power and presence. Without him I would never be on the mountain-top, I would never exit from the valley and I would never be at home in the misty flatlands that lie between. God is good; God is great! I continue to pray to see him in every day of life. May I encourage you to look daily for something where he has been real and incontrovertibly at work in your life as well?

6. Know your Achilles' heel

What do we do when the fiery darts of the enemy come? The wrong thing for a Christian to do is to duck! A soldier crouching low is far less effective than one who is standing upright (although he is a smaller target and he might be on his knees, praying!). The active response is to wield the shield of faith, putting it between our person and the fiery dart. Interestingly, the promise is that the shield will quench the darts, not just repulse them (Ephesians 6:16). Continuing the analogy of the warrior, we need to be aware of the danger of an Achilles' heel. The enemy does not spend his efforts hammering against the shield of faith if he can go straight for our weak spots. If he can bring us down with one quick shot, he will. It's simpler, it's less painful for him and he can ruin our effectiveness more quickly. There is a significant element of spiritual warfare that is no more flamboyant than this type of activity. If we know we've got particular areas of vulnerability, we need to identify them, and work at them, so that we can stay stronger for longer, and be much harder to bring down. The first stage is probably to admit to having those areas and recognise the nature of the darts. I don't know what it might be for you. It might include financial difficulties, the kids playing up or a difficult partner. It might be attitudes, thoughts or fears. I can only encourage you to specifically identify the type of attack that tends to lay you low at the first strike. Progress doesn't mean that the potential for an attack never returns; improvement consists in resorting to the promises of the cross more quickly and being able to take our place in the front line again with the minimum delay.

7. Separate temptation from thought sin

The enemy would like to confuse us with the idea that temptation and thought sin are the same thing. There are three stages to the temptation and sin process. First, we see the temptation, and if we resist it, the process stops there. The second stage would be to sin in thought but not in deed. We know that the thought is just as sinful as the act; there are six illustrations in Matthew 5 where Jesus teaches this (they all follow the format of 'You have heard it said . . . but I say to you . . .'). The final stage would be to sin in deed.

As we have said earlier in this chapter, the first stage, temptation, is part of the normal Christian life. We must not think that because we've been tempted we've necessarily sinned. It is easy to fall into some kind of guilt trip at this point. The problem starts if we slip into the second stage.

8. Don't confuse condemnation and conviction

Lastly, don't mix condemnation and conviction. One comes from the enemy, the other comes from God. They couldn't be more different. But in the middle of both activities there is a little convergent point where you're aware of something that's not quite right. From then on the paths diverge again. Conviction should lead to appropriating the grace of God to cover what's happened and to renouncing similar patterns of behaviour in the future. Condemnation takes you down into the pit again; there is no offer of a way out. We are promised that there is now no condemnation for those who are in Christ Jesus (Romans 8:1).

When I'm away preaching and other people are hosting the service, I'm very cautious about overstepping my mandate during other parts of the meeting. About fifteen years ago, there was a 'prophecy' from the back of the room during such a service. It was one of those heavy contributions – that's why I had some reservations. The message of grace, God's offer of a better alternative, was missing. This particular statement had the effect of taking people down. At the end of this so-called prophecy I felt prompted to contribute. I spoke out the verse from Romans that I've quoted above. The person who'd offered this 'prophecy' was fifty yards away from me, and he went down in the Spirit, not moving a muscle for five minutes (and these were pre-Toronto Blessing days!). I nearly joined him in surprise! Conviction and condemnation come from opposite sources and lead to very different outcomes.

Remember my original reasons for including this chapter. Unnecessarily prolonged periods down in the valley are painful and dangerous, and weaken not only yourself but the whole congregation. However, if these 'down times' are not part of your experience so far, how can you be best prepared to help others? I hope that some of these strategies and insights prove helpful.

11
Journalling

Journalling is usually defined as 'reflective writing'. It's not rocket science to conclude that we can therefore explore two aspects and sets of skills. The writing element is fairly straightforward, but reflecting deserves much more attention, and there are many interpretations about what we should focus on and how we should do it. Certainly, journalling is potentially more than keeping a diary and more than a record of prayer items or personal Bible study. The written aspect of the process helps to contribute to the discipline of reflecting regularly and properly, and enables us to look back over a period of time and be encouraged by the progress in our lives.

There is a very powerful American story often repeated in management circles that vividly illustrates the benefit of reflection. Wayne was faced with a major career decision and only knew of one consultant who could help him with this difficult choice. The consultant said that he would be happy to help, but only providing that Wayne would follow his methodology unswervingly. Reluctantly Wayne agreed, feeling that he had nowhere else to turn. The job he was considering involved a move to New York, and the consultant advised him to go and visit the prospective employer but to travel in a rather unusual way. He was to go by train, which was a couple of days' journey, rent a single sleeping compartment, and take no reading, music or writing with him. Apart from polite responses to the railway staff, he must strike up no conversations. At the end of the journey, Wayne was to telephone the consultant for further instructions. He only broke one of the rules: during the second day of the journey he asked the attendant for some paper and a pen to record some of his thoughts. When Wayne telephoned the consultant, he said, 'I now realise what you were doing. You wanted me to think things through for myself. Thank you – the answer to my career move is absolutely clear now.' The consultant laughed and replied that he had never expected that his services were going to be needed beyond that first stage. Most problems can be solved if you take some time to reflect, seek guidance and put things into perspective.

Journalling can mean whatever you want it to mean

So, the reflective element of journalling can certainly be used when we face major decisions. Following are three quotations from some very different authors, illustrating that a range of people might use a journal in other very different ways – creatively, pragmatically, for personal growth, etc.

A journal is where you practise remembering the events and meaning of the day. It is a simple instrument to help you pay attention, discern what is happening. (Anderson and Reese)

Journals are a record or landmark in the redemptive process. They keep us accountable on a daily basis, expectant and watchful for redemptive possibilities in each new day. And so our journal will contain a blend of discovery. It is a safe place to do exploration, shed our misconceptions, reclaim our lost or forgotten parts, recover the fragments that living makes of us at times, and cultivate the gift of new life. In this way journal writing becomes a viable prayer form, and our journal becomes our own book of psalms. (Jana Rea)

A journal is a means of confirming a decision, reminding us of past guidance when times were difficult, of God's love and goodness, of blessing experienced. It is a means of listening to God, a tool for growth. (Ann England)

Possible reasons for journalling

In addition to the various purposes illustrated above, here is a summary of the main reasons I have met for keeping a journal. They are culled from a variety of sources and adapted.

1. An aid to mentoring. Disciples may make a journal to record their responses and reflections on various projects and tasks, particularly areas where they may be 'stuck' or repeatedly struggling. The journal can be used to highlight any aspects of life and ministry they are dealing with in mentoring sessions. This is probably the only aspect where journalling *might* contribute to discipling rather than discipleship. It's the only situation where I would recommend that a disciple *may* share aspects of their journal.

2. Increased understanding of self. A journal can help us to recognise who we were and where we've been on our

pilgrimage. John Mallison says, 'self-knowledge leads to humility, which is the key to swing wide the door of our lives to God's love.' Back in Chapter 7, we highlighted that self-awareness is an important part of emotional intelligence. A few people have said to me that a journal has led to a much greater degree of self-acceptance – loving yourself better. Remember the commandment to love thy neighbour as thyself.

3. Enhancing personal devotions. A journal can be a record of our spiritual journey.

4. Guidance and making decisions. Some people limit their journalling to significant revelations, including visions, dreams and prophetic encounters. For folk who find long-term issues difficult, this is a worthwhile, but not too demanding, exercise. Referring back to the contents of the journal is then a reminder of the significant and pivotal moments that have given them a sense of direction.

5. Adding meaning to everyday life. A journal can help us to make 'connections' with our past and make sense of our lives. Ken Gire says, 'The purpose of a journal is to help us live deliberately.' People who use a journal for this reason have said that they gained a fuller understanding of continuity.

6. The emotional life. Some people use a journal to write about their responses to their world. The emphasis would be on feelings and interpretation, not just a history of events. Journalling can be particularly effective when done as a means of working through issues like a relationship breakdown, loss or pain, such as bereavement. All, or any combination, of these limited applications are perfectly valid.

7. Increased learning. 'Journalling introduces the important aspect of autobiography into learning experiences, personalising the learning, strengthening the ownership of the experience and the awareness of its relevance for future action' (John Mallison). My wife, Vicky, found a journal especially helpful after some counselling training; she used the journal to record examples of when she had applied what she had recently learned.

8. Linking vision and time management. A journal can help to show us where we are going and what is driving us there. Some people find it encouraging to write down the specific actions that have been achieved in the day or week. Vision and time management go together in a way – the long- and short-term approaches to life. Just as some busy people need help to hold on to a vision (number 4 above), so other folk struggle to translate big dreams into action. The positive discipline of recorded goal-setting can prove an aid.

9. Working through problems. A journal can bring illumination and revelation. One anonymous writer said: 'Writing a journal is like watching a Polaroid snapshot develop before your eyes. It can help create clarity in a given situation.'

10. Joy and gratitude. Journalling can bring a greater awareness of daily life, an extra dimension of appreciation and thankfulness to God. On a personal note, this level of reflection has been the greatest benefit to me. My life is pretty consistent, but not as full of joy as I would like. I have found that reflecting each day on the things that gave me reason for thanksgiving has made a considerable difference.

Let's just revisit some of the key comments at the beginning of this chapter. Journalling is reflective writing; we can improve the writing component, but what we reflect on and how we reflect are probably the most significant issues. The written element can be used to enhance our thinking and reflecting on any combination of the above reasons for journalling. All of them, however, can be made into constructive tools without a written record. So if you are considering starting a journal, you need to decide *what* you want it to achieve before considering *how* to set about it. The purpose must precede the method if you are going to sustain the practice in the dull or busy seasons.

Practical hints for journalling

Like learning, not all journalling is the same. It's personal and unique. Your style may well change and develop. Be patient, as it can take time to develop journal-writing. Some people write lots, others little; some frequently, others infrequently. Some people prefer to use a book, some prefer to use a computer. Be aware of the options and come to your own decisions.

1. Think about the frequency. Do it regularly. Have a regular routine, be it daily or weekly, and it will end up being habit forming! If you follow this practice, the patterns of your life will emerge in your writing. Find the best time of day to do it. Find out what works for you – right time, right place, right style!
2. Let it flow. Tristine Rainer in *The New Diary* says, 'Write fast, write everything, include everything, write from your feelings, write from your body, and accept whatever comes.'

Write what comes into your mind without concern about its literary quality or analysis. Write spontaneously but thoughtfully. Tell it like it is.

3. Remember that it's personal. Confidentiality and privacy are vital if a journal is going to be honest and real. You may need an agreement of confidentiality with others in your home. Keep your journal in a safe place where others do not easily access it. If it's not confidential, you're bound to feel less free to be candid. A journal without personal honesty doesn't work at all. As we have said previously, you may agree to share some of the contents with your mentor, but make sure that such sharing is on your terms entirely. The danger is that a small improvement in the mentoring process is paid for by losing most of the benefits of journalling.

4. Include feelings and interpretation. Among all the possible scenarios for keeping a journal that we have talked about earlier, in my view the need for it to be more than just a diary is non-negotiable. Gordon MacDonald has said:

> Into the journal went words describing my feelings, my fear, my sense of weakness, my hopes and discoveries about where Christ was leading me. When I felt empty or defeated I talked about that too in my journal. Slowly I began to realise that the journal was helping me to come to grips with an enormous part of my inner person that I had never been fully honest about. No longer could fears and struggles remain inside without definition.

Feelings are based on previous experience. Feelings alter future actions. We need to know *what* we feel before we can explore *why* we feel it. Record your feelings, how you are *really* feeling! Don't repress or hide negative feelings – own

them. God already knows about them. Include both negative and positive feelings.

5. Use 'I' language. Write in the first person singular. It's
about you and your life, no one else's. It's not meant for
anyone else.

6. Review regularly. I was struck recently by the regular use of
the word 'remember' in Scripture (161 times). Part of the
benefit of journalling lies in the discipline of writing things
down, but the next stage is to read over our memories from
time to time. We need to build in a regular review of what
we have written and search for meaning. Plan action within
the review. What am I going to do about what I have
written? Is the journalling yielding the maximum for me?

7. Consider possible proformas. Dramatic improvements in
software mean that for people who prefer to journal on the
computer, it is very easy to create a proforma for each contribution. If we reach a settled style, the computer offers real
advantages in regenerating the same layout. Another alternative is to use a ring-binder and photocopy a prepared outline.
Here are three suggestions to use as a standard model:

  (a) Ken Gire, in his book *The Reflective Life*, says there are
  three central aspects that might be addressed whenever
  you make an entry:

   (i) Read the moment   What actually happened?
   (ii) Reflect on the moment   What did it mean?
   (iii) Respond to the   How can I apply what I
         moment   have learnt?

  (b) Ignatian spirituality speaks of the four laws of reflection. They too could be the basis of a routine:

   (i) 'Look back' (memory): Look back over the
       day/week with God in mind. What have I missed
       of God's activity?

(ii) 'Look through' (thinking): Make connections with what has happened. What is 'of God'? What patterns emerge?

(iii) 'Look forward' (imagination): What ideas or goals come out of my reflection? How should I change? What should I do differently?

(iv) 'Look around' (community): What are the implications for my family and friends? How can I learn from them?

(c) Chuck Swindoll recommends these questions:

- What am I trusting God for today?
- What are the joys and stresses in my key relationships now?
- In what ways am I experiencing inner peace? How am I lacking?
- What are my three most significant prayer requests?
- Am I entertaining any fears at the moment? What are they?
- Is there any measure of discontent? Describe it.
- What has made me laugh recently?

The possible benefits of journalling

Here are a few comments from people who say that they have benefited from journalling. One is indirect, but the other three are from colleagues and friends who have regularly used a journal.

Did you realise that people who regularly keep a notebook, journal or diary find it a powerful stress release and it can lead to immunity from illness? They are less likely to suffer from depression and many other ailments. Psychologists have suggested that it is the 'disclosure' aspect of journaling, the confession that does this. (From the clinical research of James Pennebaker of the University of Texas in his book *Opening Up: The healing power of expressing emotions*, and quoted in an article in the *Sunday Times*)

Journalling has helped to bring self-awareness and realisation to me. Lights have dawned as to why I am like I am, what are the 'cycles of offending behaviour' that I struggle with and how I can deny them room to operate in my life.

I am now more aware of trigger points in my life, of the reasons I get angry or irrational. I try to build strategies to avoid them.

My journal is a reminder to me of my dreams, what God is saying to me. It holds me accountable to my goals and my aspirations. I review my journal in the light of these to see what progress I've made (if any).

I must come clean (rather late in the day, you probably think). I do not complete a journal regularly myself. Why don't I? I think that there can only be one possible answer for someone who has heard and read about the potential of journalling: at present I don't believe that, for me, the advantages outweigh the effort. Much of the first-hand work in this chapter comes from Tony Horsfall, Director of the Equip training pro-gramme at Bawtry Hall, and Jonathan Dunning, leader of Meadowhead Christian Fellowship in Sheffield. Both are excellent men who live what they teach, and I gladly acknowl-edge their generosity in sharing their research and experiences.

However, I don't totally feel a fraud in constructing this chapter! Although I don't undertake the written element of journalling, and therefore miss the possible advantages of continuity and review, I do reflect – not just by navel-gazing, but in a regular and disciplined manner. The literature and teaching around journalling has greatly sharpened this process. My testimony would be about the increase in joy in my life as a direct result of disciplined thanksgiving, the development of the gratitude attitude! I leave you to make the following decisions:

Questions

- How significant is reflection to my learning?
- From the lists earlier in this chapter, in what ways could a journal serve me and enhance my discipleship?
- Would I work more readily with a notebook or on the computer?
- If I chose not to do a journal regularly at this juncture, in what particular short-term situations might I try this approach and find benefits?
- What is my alternative to journalling?

12

Influencing

Discipling, coaching and mentoring all seek changes in beliefs, attitudes and behaviour. The 'senior partner' is therefore trying to influence the disciple. We can attempt to influence people in a variety of ways. Good people-developers recognise that there are many arrows in the quiver called influencing, and try to use a wide range on different occasions. In this chapter I want to explore these options because when we are conscious of the possibilities, we are more likely to be flexible in our approach and successful in the outcome. We are basically asking the questions: 'When I believe I'm right, how do I get a hearing? On what basis should I appeal to the disciple?'

Some of you might be suspicious that I am really talking about manipulation. I sincerely believe this is not the case. First, manipulation is underhand and covert, whereas what we are attempting is open and above board. Second, we are right to be seeking change in the disciples' lives. The biblical injunction is to 'make' disciples, teaching them to obey; it's a very positive and active verb. Remember a key statement from earlier in the book: discipling is both relational and purposeful.

Sometimes the failure to get the most obvious (so we think!) suggestions adopted is the lack of patience shown by the influencer. The simplest ideas are often only manifestations of deeper attitudes, and for the learner to make an apparently easy improvement requires challenging far more basic premisses. Don't forget, if people make two or three significant changes per year, they have done well.

Influencing is a process, not just an event

Events are frequently of short duration; processes usually take more time. It takes times to build up trust so that our motives are recognised as being consistent, reliable and 'other-oriented'. It takes time to understand the nature of the blockages before we give advice. Sometimes the disciple is not emotionally prepared to pay the price of a change, and there generally is a price, even if it is only about relinquishing the familiar!

Possibly the least effective approach to influencing is to rely upon the power invested in the position. We have already said that we are all called to make disciples and relatively few people are in leadership positions. So there must be a rich variety of alternative approaches for disciplers, coaches and mentors to consider. The sociologist Max Weber focused on a useful distinction. He separated power (*macht* in the German language, best translated as 'might') and authority (which cannot be imposed and can only be accorded to you). Positional power is like soap: it's slippery and the more you use it, the quicker it runs out! Be reluctant to wield the bulk of the clout that comes with position. Sometimes it is not the attitude of the leader that is the problem; members can put leaders on pedestals and be too keen to please authority figures. Whatever the reason, if a disciple adopts a suggestion from a leader simply because the source was a leader, then the outcome is closer to compliant behaviour than a fundamental heart and attitude change. In the remainder of this chapter, we will be assuming 'horizontal influencing' with no hierarchical context.

Influencing styles

Please complete the following questionnaire now, which will help us explore your preferences in influencing. Score each of these statements according to the following code:

If you do this very frequently	Score 3 points
If you do this quite often	Score 2 points
If you do this less than most other people	Score 1 point
If you do this rarely or never	Score 0 points

When I am trying to influence a person's beliefs, behaviour or attitudes . . .

1. I come up with new lines of reasoning to persuade people who disagree with my ideas.

   ___

2. I give information of a personal nature that reveals my inner feelings.

   ___

3. I let others know when my requirements are not met.

   ___

4. I openly sympathise with others when they have problems.

   ___

5. I let people know when I simply appreciate them for who they are.

   ___

6. I am known as a very positive and optimistic person.

7. I will use any, or all, legitimate means to get things done.

8. My plans are designed to maximise the gifts in other people.

9. I generate a feeling of 'We're in this together' among colleagues.

10. I give firm advice based on my own experience.

11. I give authority as well as jobs when I delegate.

12. I listen carefully for long periods without interrupting.

13. I build strong relationships with people before attempting to challenge them.

14. I use emotionally charged language to generate and sustain enthusiasm.

15. When I want something, I will pressurise others into giving it.

16. I adapt my plans when I notice that people are under pressure.

17. I communicate my passion about the value and importance of the common task.

18. I have strong views about the right way of doing things.

19. I give people lots of freedom to make their own decisions.

20. I put together a sound logical argument.

21. I accept criticism without becoming defensive.

22. I readily give credit for good work.

___

23. I use open or veiled threats to get compliance.

___

24. I have lots of patience with those who are wary of change.

___

25. I use group dynamics to bring enhanced ownership of our plans.

___

26. I use statements like 'If I were you . . .'.

___

27. I treat other people as being worthy of my trust and confidence.

___

28. I am creative in producing supportive evidence for my proposals.

___

29. I am open about my own unfulfilled hopes and fears.

___

30. I can appear judgemental to others.

___

31. I can comfortably handle extreme expressions of feelings and emotion from others.

___

32. I am just as ready to affirm the person as I am to credit good performance.

___

33. I bring others to see the exciting possibilities and potential in a situation.

___

34. I encourage people to produce their own solutions to problems.

___

35. I clarify standards that I think other people ought to meet.

___

36. I stress common values and aims that strengthen people's commitment to one another.

___

37. I have found that people turn to me when they have problems.

          ___

38. I am willing to use 'give and take' as a means to an end.

          ___

39. I not only lead from the front, I take others with me.

          ___

40. I recognise that high self-esteem is a prerequisite of change.

          ___

41. I give feedback to show that I have been listening.

          ___

42. I have strong views about right and wrong, and make them known.

          ___

43. I readily admit my own mistakes and deficiencies.

          ___

44. I defend my own ideas robustly.

          ___

45. Friendship is ultimately more important than progress.

          ___

46. I frequently share with great excitement about the vision for the future.

          ___

47. I solve differences in goals and interests by negotiation and bargaining.

          ___

48. I give additional time to people who need emotional support.

          ___

49. I cause others to see how they can achieve more by working together.

          ___

50. I use moral imperatives such as 'should', 'ought' and 'must'.

          ___

51. I look for ways to incorporate other people's ideas and suggestions.

          ___

52. When people have objections to my viewpoint, I am quick with counter-arguments.

___

53. I acknowledge when I am confused, uncertain or don't have the answer.

___

54. I make moral judgements about the contributions of others.

___

55. I listen carefully when people express views different from my own.

___

56. I help other people feel that they have a worthwhile contribution to make.

___

57. I know what I want others to do.

___

58. I raise others' recognition of the benefits of pulling together.

___

59. In my planning, I take full account of the stress that people are under.

___

60. I use inducements and rewards to get results.

___

61. My enthusiasm carries people forward when the going gets tough.

___

62. I have sustained relationships long after I have formally discipled people.

___

63. During discussions, I summarise or paraphrase what others have said to make sure they have been heard.

___

64. I show my approval when others do well.

___

65. I admit my lack of knowledge and skill in a particular situation.

___

66. I draw attention to the flaws in others' ideas or reasoning.

___

Add together your scores for questions	Total score	Title of influencing approach
1, 20, 28, 44, 52, 66		Logic
2, 21, 29, 43, 53, 65		Disclosure
3, 22, 30, 42, 54, 64		Evaluation
4, 12, 31, 41, 55, 63		Listening
5, 13, 32, 40, 45, 62		Affirmation
6, 14, 33, 39, 46, 61		Enthusiasm
7, 15, 23, 38, 47, 60		Bargaining
8, 16, 24, 37, 48, 59		Support
9, 17, 25, 36, 49, 58		Group synergy
10, 18, 26, 35, 50, 57		Direction/guidance
11, 19, 27, 34, 51, 56		Autonomy

Your raw scores are relatively unimportant, as some people award points frugally, while others strew them about like confetti! I suggest that you pay particular attention to the three lowest totals and try to use them more when you attempt to influence people. Your highest four totals (and some scores may be equal) are probably your present active approaches. Here is a fuller explanation of each of the styles:

1. The logical approach

The logical influencer tries for success by painting the rational argument. This approach is commonly used by left-brain thinkers. Frequently used phrases include 'It stands to reason that . . .' and 'You know it makes sense' (as often heard on the TV series *Only Fools and Horses*!). It is often hard to spontaneously counter the proverbial wordsmith, but an apparently won debate seldom produces change. It's important to have alternative influencing styles to hand, because people using this style can easily get frustrated if the other party goes round in circles. It's much better to try other optional styles than to push harder.

2. Personal disclosure

I have found that some leaders particularly are slow to use this very effective approach. Folk with an apparently strong self-image are sometimes reluctant to put their own weaknesses on the table, but an expression of our own humanity can often move the influencing process forward. Showing vulnerability does not cause people to trample over you. Statements like 'I've had difficulty with that myself' or 'I could do with your help on this one' are hard to resist. I have difficulty with the school of thought that discourages comments and revelations about yourself, but the danger of transferring the focus onto the influencer for too long is very real; don't go into too much detail.

3. Evaluative contributions

Listen for statements like 'That won't work, you know' and 'If you do X, then Y will happen'. Clear thinkers who believe they have considerable insight can resort to this style too readily. Their comments are often designed to prevent other people from falling flat on their faces, but sometimes people need to press ahead and be free to make their own mistakes – falling on your face can be highly educational! There's nothing like experience. Despite good intentions and motives, the tone of voice that often accompanies evaluative comments can easily be interpreted as 'talking down'.

Another, more positive, aspect of evaluation concerns feed-back. When a person who is seen as competent tells a task-oriented person how to improve further, that can be very motivational.

4. Listening

Never underestimate the power of simply listening. It's pivotal to asking the right questions, but it also shows that you value the person. It gives the opportunity to find the blockage that is preventing a course of action. There is a big message in showing that the disciple is worth a good hearing; you are recognising that their standpoint is valid for them! Resist the temptation to jump in and give them a word of advice. Quite often people will think as they talk, and just by listening you are helping them to formulate conclusions. As we have said before, people are far more likely to do what *they* say rather than what *you* tell them!

5. Affirmation

The desire to be liked and popular is there in all of us, and very strong in some people. Acceptance is more important to them than the knowledge that a task has been done well. A comment like 'I really enjoyed your company at our meeting last week' or 'Our friendship is important to me' needs to be genuine, but can also be very effective in building relationship and hence causing change. A more negative slant on the same theme means that action can be provoked in other people, but purely out of their desire to please the influencer. The Tupperware sales technique has exploited this very fully; people buy the products to please the hostess. Affirmation is a sharp weapon, and as with most of the other approaches, it can be a dangerous toy.

6. Enthusiasm

When we are in the discipling business it's great to have a few people around who see the cup as half-full rather than half-empty – the eternal optimists! Real enthusiasm is infectious and carries other people forward when there is a tendency towards faint-heartedness. It's amazing what heights we can scale when somebody else sincerely believes we can do it, and tells us so. The people who use this style are often extroverts with high energy levels; nothing fazes them.

7. Bargaining

One of the most widespread components of human nature is the concept of reciprocity. People will try to make some form of repayment for what another person has provided. Because the receiver is under such a heavy obligation, we can give, confident that there is no loss, as there will be an act of repayment later. For example, having been invited for a meal with friends, there is a strong expectation of a return invitation. In bargaining, the rule is just as powerful, even if the first favour was not requested. Perhaps surprisingly, this phenomenon works in discipling as much as in any other area of life. We will encourage people to take action by simply doing something for them.

8. Support

The greater the challenge, the more we need support. Being chucked in at the deep end without a rubber ring produces feelings of loneliness, isolation and vulnerability. Comments like 'I'll be right there with you' and 'Let me know when you need a hand' can be very reassuring. To make sure we pitch our support levels appropriately, a question like 'What help do you want from me?' leads to a greater understanding and helps us to make sure that we don't force too much help onto people when they don't want it.

9. Group synergy

The essence of this style of influencing appeals strongly to people who like working in teams. We can stress both the fun of togetherness and the potential for improved results. For some people, the sense of corporate responsibility is very strong. The prospect of failure does not galvanise them into more action, but letting their mates down is much more serious. There is a strong emphasis on the future in this style and it often looks at the long-term potential mutual benefits, two great characteristics.

10. Direction/guidance

People who have a strong preference for this style are not slow in giving advice. They will use statements like 'If I were in your shoes . . .' or 'What you ought to do is . . .'. Often the style shows a measure of impatience and in general is not very effective, so 'if I were you', I wouldn't use it very often!

11. Autonomy

In this style, the influencer gives the disciple a great deal of scope. The learner is encouraged to try things, make their own decisions, and fall or stand by the outcomes. Welcome to the biggest room in the world – room for improvement! The oversight of the influencer is the lowest in this style. Leaders who see themselves as pace-setters have a strong preference for this approach as they don't need to spend too long monitoring the development of other people.

Very early in this chapter, I raised a serious concern – that conscious influencing could be interpreted as manipulation. Yet discipling calls for us to help people change, so herein lies the tension. The prime reason for a failure to improve our influencing skills revolves around this concern. In Chapter 7, we referred to the dark side of the power motive drive. The temptation to manipulate will always be there for people with a high score in this drive, but that same high score can be used positively to help people. We won't improve our management of this drive by refusing to explore it.

Questions

- How effective are your current efforts at influencing?
- What can you do to make yourself more credible?
- How can you make your messages more persuasive?
- Which style has surprised you most by its potential?

13

The Good Disciple

The bulk of this book has focused on the 'senior' party, the discipler, whether their role is coaching, mentoring or a blend. With their additional experience comes a substantial responsibility for the discipling process, as well as a mutual responsibility for the outcomes. Yet we also need to focus on the qualities and attributes of the classic disciple. Ultimately their future fulfilment is at stake and it would be wrong to minimise the contribution that they have to make to the partnership.

Discipleship is first about individually following the person of Jesus Christ. There is no alternative to the practice of the devotional life. Nobody else can feed on the word or commune with God for us. We may need help from time to time in understanding what is written, but only the disciple can put the hours in. A personal relationship with God has to be just that; there can be no substitute. My next core expectation of a disciple is that they will work at relationships, because our faith is worked out by our interaction and integration with the rest of the body of Christ. That's the acid test of the biblical theory.

I now want to consider some qualities of the good disciple that might be slightly less obvious at first glance.

Good disciples must be prepared to question, and change, their deepest beliefs

As we have already mentioned in Chapter 1, Jesus challenged the deepest beliefs of the disciples. Some of the challenges came through what he said, others by what he did. Here are another five examples:

- His disciples return and are surprised to find him talking to a woman (John 4:27).
- Jesus washes the disciples' feet: 'Unless I wash you, you have no part with me' (John 13:5–8).
- The astonishment of the disciples that it is easier for a camel to go through the eye of a needle than for a rich man to enter the kingdom of God (Matthew 19:24).
- The importance of children (Matthew 18:2, 5, 10).
- Peter encourages Jesus not to go to Jerusalem. He replies, 'Get behind me, Satan! You are a stumbling-block to me; you do not have in mind the things of God, but the things of men' (Matthew 16:23).

In today's language, we could say that Jesus challenged their paradigms. While they were quite shocked, the incidents did not result in a breakdown of relationship or the end of their discipling. We should be looking for the same qualities in today's disciples. Sometimes challenges will go to the very core of their belief systems. This is not an initial test of discipling necessarily, but it is likely to occur sometime. I think that we have probably defined 'teachable' by looking at this quality. A disciple who says that they are prepared to change, but in practice that means 'only within existing paradigms', is applying crippling boundaries to their development.

A disciple's thinking should go through the following six discrete stages:

1. The event or conversation.
2. Their own inner dialogue about the event.
3. Their emotional reaction to the event.
4. Possibly a continued dialogue with other people.
5. A review of their paradigm, possibly establishing a new one.
6. A change of behaviour in the light of the new paradigm.

Good disciples do not stop after stage three!

Good disciples develop a close relationship with their coach/mentor

In my ideal world, structure would not be so important, and all disciples would have the freedom to work with the range of inputs that suits them best. The real world is less capable of delivering the perfect situation for all disciples, partly because some disciplers would be too busy! Nevertheless, as we have emphasised in Chapter 6, trust will be the limiting factor that defines the ceiling of the discipling process. There will always be two perspectives on a relationship, and to produce effective discipling we should not minimise the validity of the disciple's standpoint. Obviously, if a disciple finds most relationships difficult, especially with people who desire change in their lives, then serious questions have to be asked about their attitude!

So I want to be realistic about discipling *relationships*. I do not expect a disciple (or a discipler!) to score 100 per cent on vulnerability, teachability, submissiveness, faithfulness and obedience, but I do require that a disciple can find some people to whom they can frequently exhibit these qualities. However non-directive the process and style of the discipler, disciples must be responsive and respectful to the suggestions of that discipler.

In time, disciples must be prepared to come to a clearly defined aim as to what they want from the relationship. Frequently, initial meetings may be substantially exploratory, but soon a sense of direction must emerge. I have certainly found that my greatest development has come when I knew what I wanted to learn. One significant lesson came very easily. I have a very high regard for a particular church leader, formerly a solicitor, who is also very imaginative and spontaneous. Having listened to him and watched his ministry on various occasions, I asked him for some time together. It transpired that the quality of his devotional life and preparation for every ministry appointment was of a very high order. You can be spontaneous when your options are thoroughly prepared and at your fingertips, and when you are close to God. The point is that my learning was very deliberate; I knew that I had seen something worthwhile. Unusually, the theoretical understanding took place very quickly.

A final quality encapsulated within the relationship is also critical. How does the mentor see the disciple? What potential have they identified? In many small ways, the mentor will communicate these messages and they will have an impact on the disciple. As Maxwell puts it: 'People tend to become what the most important people in their lives think they will become' (*Developing the Leader within You*, p.116). Eventually, however, the receiver of communications confers the meaning. It is the disciple's understanding of the mentor's view that will drive the relationship.

Good disciples must handle failure well

Again, I want to try to put an unusual slant on some very obvious qualities. It would be easy to say that perseverance, resilience and 'stickability' are vital characteristics of good disciples. When are these features manifest? Certainly not when life is plain sailing. Only when we encounter discouragement, rejection, failure and persecution are we likely to give up. Overcoming such problems is stressful at the time, but ultimately those incidents bring the encouragement of significant progress. The real test of a disciple's attitudes is when we *fail* to overcome these hurdles. Can we take it on the chin? Are we capable of getting up, dusting ourselves down, striding out afresh and experiencing the grace of God? Here are a few quotations in fairly frequent use that illustrate what we should be looking for:

- 'The brightest dawn comes after the darkest night.'
- 'Most people give up a few maddening steps from their goal.'
- 'With every failure comes the seed of opportunity.'
- 'The only failure is someone who has given up.'

Sometimes, coping with failure is largely a pride issue. I regard one of my greatest strengths to be in analysis of situations, clear thinking and logical evaluation. At one point, I made a very poor career move when I gravely misjudged the quality of an organisation and some of its key players. In retrospect, many years later, the hardest consequence was learning to trust my own critical faculties again. The biggest battle was in my own mind.

I wonder if Peter was ever discouraged in a similar way. His impetuous streak contributed to some real clangers. There are many examples, like when he walked on water, when he didn't want Jesus to wash his feet, and ultimately when he denied Jesus. Why was Peter a specially chosen disciple? There were probably many reasons, but partly, I believe, it was because he could handle failure.

Good disciples must accept the responsibility for their own situation

I frequently come across one big fallacy that inhibits personal development more than many other barriers. We need to be able to learn from both success and failure, and perhaps there are more lessons intrinsic to our failures if we could access them. There is a certain mentality that underpins this learning: it's the difference between ownership and blame. People who attribute their failures to other people and external causes are not in a position to consider improvements. Suppose the church summer fête is unsuccessful, by common agreement. The co-ordinator could say:

- 'It was the poor weather.'
- 'The congregation couldn't be bothered.'
- 'I didn't get the full support of the other leaders.'
- 'It's just bad luck that the Baptists had an event on that same Saturday.'

Or they might say:

- 'I shouldn't have picked a date in May. It's too early for the best weather.'
- 'I should have approached more key people and enlisted their help.'
- 'I could have asked other churches about their dates via the fraternal meeting.'

The key thing with attribution is that we have a choice about how we view the causes of our successes and failures. In order to benefit from experiences, we need to choose reasons within our control.

There is a second dimension of attribution if we seek to gain perspectives on causes. If we see failures as caused by internal but also static reasons, that's a bad combination. It opens us to serious condemnation, because what we are saying is, 'It's my fault and I cannot do anything about it. That quality is fixed within me.' I believe that this is the single main reason why people are reluctant to accept responsibility when things go wrong. It's a defence mechanism against owning static weaknesses. The characteristic words are 'always' and 'never'. Listen carefully for statements like:

- 'I've never been good at administration.'
- 'I've always been late with things.'
- 'I've never been able to take others with me.'

We must immediately challenge the implied 'fixedness' of these causes.

Good disciples must be committed to continuous learning and prepared for change

Good disciples are hungry. They want more of God and want to do great things for him. They already have a track record of growth and personal development. As a prospective mentor, you will find it much easier to deal with an excess of ambition than to handle stagnation and complacency. If the potential disciple is inclined to cruise through life, varying between second and third gear, they don't want or need your time and experience.

Potential disciples should already be exhibiting these qualities of hunger and passion before we offer to give them our best. Are they showing signs of proactivity, self-discipline and a proven track record of change? Even new Christians should be able to give an encouraging answer to some of these questions, even if some of the responses are from their 'previous' life:

- What have you been reading recently?
- What courses have you been on?
- What have you learned in this role?
- What have you learned in the last month?
- What has God been saying to you recently?

If there is no existing track record in some of these areas, I seriously question the disciple's motives in desiring our input. We must make sure that the limited physical and emotional resources that we have available go into people who truly want to grow. There is the possibility that we legitimise the disciple's passive lifestyle by association.

Good disciples are goal-centred

Some Christians have a strong aversion to goal-setting. I suspect that their reasons are that in areas like pastoral care and worship they feel measurable outcomes are inappropriate. Generally there's something of avoidance in taking this stance. I'm not suggesting that we set goals in every area of possible activity and on every occasion, but goal orientation in most of what we do is critical to personal development. It's the basic building block of both time and change management. The Japanese motto, 'If you can't measure it, you can't manage it', is absolutely right. People who set goals achieve more, grow more and gain more satisfaction than their counterparts. If disciples are simply goal averse, discipling is limited. You cannot prescribe and meet goals on their behalf.

Good disciples define their ultimate expectation

What does God want them to become? What does he want them to do? At what level can we be satisfied as disciplers? And therefore what can we hope for in the people we disciple? In various parts of the New Testament, we are encouraged to *aim* for perfection:

Aim for perfection, listen to my appeal, be of one mind, live in peace. (2 Corinthians 13:11)

'Be perfect, therefore, as your heavenly Father is perfect.' (Matthew 5:48)

'If you want to be perfect, go, sell your possessions and give to the poor, and you will have treasure in heaven.' (To the rich young ruler in Matthew 19:21)

> We are glad whenever we are weak but you are strong; and our
> prayer is for your perfection. (2 Corinthians 13:9)

The Greek word for perfection translates more accurately as 'to make adequate' or 'to make completely effective' (Hewitt, in the Tyndale commentaries). Vine adds the dimensions of 'having reached the end' and 'finished'. Full growth and maturity are additional slants on a word that is not easily translated by a single word in English. The normal use of the word is not a complete reflection of the biblical meaning. Our concept of perfection is often crippling, not inspirational, because it is limited. 'To all perfection I see a limit; but your commands are boundless' (Psalm 119:96).

Good disciples keep on keeping on

I believe that faith, righteousness and perseverance are very close together. They may sound very different words and concepts, but in the outworking, their proximity is more obvious. One of my favourite verses, found initially in Genesis, is also quoted in three New Testament books: 'Abram believed the Lord, and he credited it to him as righteousness' (Genesis 15:6; Romans 4:3; Galatians 3:6; James 2:23). It doesn't say that Abram believed *in* God, but that he believed God.

If you're going to believe someone you have to hear them before you take their word at face value or choose to disagree with them. I can believe in someone, but I don't necessarily have to accept what they are saying; that's completely different. If believing was deemed righteousness for Abram, then I reckon that the same measure applies to us. If we believe God, and walk in the steps that he tells us, believing will mean doing as well as hearing. If I've not been deflected from that path, that's the essence of victory on a day-to-day basis. The prime criterion for being a disciple of Jesus is to hear him and then to obey him. As J. Dwight Pentecost said, 'It does not take much of a man to be a disciple, but it takes all of him that there is' (*Design for Discipleship*, p. 39).

I've never experienced this, but I wonder how soldiers feel at the end of a war. I imagine that there would be a whole range of very mixed emotions. Possibly they would take time to relax after the intensity of the stress level. I'm not sure that the main feeling would be simple elation and the joy of victory. Perhaps the greatest sensation would be relief, the knowledge of survival. I imagine that there would be great sadness for friends and companions who had suffered or died during the war. Perhaps there would be some compassion for the innocent victims. There might be a sense of a job well done, knowing that there had been a faithful response when duty had called.

I believe that we experience some similar feelings in our spiritual battles. There are times when we are out of the front line, in reserve and re-equipping. On active duty, and in a war zone, vigilance is key, and we also have a prowling enemy. But at the end of our spiritual battle, there will be great elation.

I remember two famous Olympic athletes and how they handled major injuries in their races. The incident in which Zola Budd and Mary Decker-Slaney clashed, and Decker-Slaney fell, took place in the 3,000 metres race in the 1984 Olympic Games in Los Angeles. The two were among the favourites for the title. Mary Decker-Slaney had almost film-star fame as the all-American woman competing against a Czech woman suspected of taking steroids. Zola Budd was notorious for having taken British citizenship in order to avoid the ban on South African competitors because of apartheid, and because she was young, largely self-trained and ran barefoot. Zola finished the race in seventh place. There was much press speculation about whether Decker-Slaney's injury was as serious as she gave the impression at the time. (Summarised from *Sporting Females* by Jennifer Hargreaves.)

By contrast, the second incident, involving Derek Redmond, was in the semi-final of the 400 metres at the Olympic Games in Barcelona in 1992. He had been fighting injury prior to the games but was determined to qualify and compete. His hamstring went during the race and he had to pull up. People went to his aid, but he pushed them away so as not to be disqualified, and tried to complete the race. Again he collapsed and his father came from the crowd to help him over the line. His father said afterwards that he knew it would disqualify Derek but he also knew how much it meant to him to finish. Redmond received acclaim for his determination and fortitude in adversity (*IOC Official Olympic Companion*, 1996).

I think that there is a legitimate spiritual parallel here. When we reach the end of our earthly race, it would be good to say that we've breasted the tape, ideally going strong, and with confidence. There's an obvious link to perseverance. There is a great weight of Scripture around instructions like:

- persevere
- press on
- keep on (52 references)
- continue (61 references)

For example:

> You need to persevere so that when you have done the will of God, you will receive what he has promised. (Hebrews 10:36)

Watch your life and doctrine closely. Persevere in them, because if you do, you will save both yourself and your hearers. (1 Timothy 4:16)

Not that I have already obtained all this, or have already been made perfect, but I press on to take hold of that for which Christ Jesus took hold of me. (Philippians 3:12)

I press on towards the goal to win the prize for which God has called me heavenwards in Christ Jesus. (Philippians 3:14)

He will keep you strong to the end, so that you will be blameless on the day of our Lord Jesus Christ. (1 Corinthians 1:8)

Keep on loving each other as brothers. (Hebrews 13:1)

Continue to work out your salvation with fear and trembling. (Philippians 2:12)

Continue in your faith, established and firm. (Colossians 1:23)

Continue to live in him, rooted and built up in him, strengthened in the faith as you were taught, and overflowing with thankfulness. (Colossians 2:6)

Continue to do the things we command. (2 Thessalonians 3:4)

Continue to walk in the truth. (3 John 3)

Let him who does right continue to do right; and let him who is holy continue to be holy. (Revelation 22:11b)

Conclusion

Please remember that the majority of this book is focused on the discipling process and how disciplers can become more effective in those relationships. This chapter offers the principal balance and puts the spotlight on the disciple. There is no substitute for discipleship, actively and personally fostering our own walk with God. As I said at the outset, we need both discipleship and discipling. My experience is that effective discipling stands or falls on the issue of the heart of the disciple.

14

The Climate of the Learning Church

I often quote the statistical insight that 'up to 90 per cent of an individual's effectiveness is dependent not on their own efforts, but on the corporate culture'. I wish I could find the exact book and page reference again, but I know it must be true because I read it in print! There is wide research about the importance of the corporate culture on performance although, in fairness, I do quote the highest result I've seen because of the impact during seminar presentations.

Suppose for a moment that I am guilty of quoting a wild over-statement (perish the thought!). Suppose that only 50 per cent of our effectiveness is determined by the corporate culture. It would still mean that a study and knowledge of the culture of an individual church would be as critical towards discipleship as the rest of this and similar books put together. Good coaches and mentors must have a clear understanding of the impact of the positive and negative features of the church culture.

There is no point in being too technical unless that brings additional benefits, so I am going to use the terms 'culture', 'climate' and 'ethos' interchangeably, despite the fact that there are nuances between them. Essentially for me they all mean 'The way we do things here'. Values are a parallel concept and they can be defined as the guiding principles that govern our behaviour. Perhaps we could say that the corporate culture is the organisational behaviour as a result of the core values in action.

Let me try to illustrate the impact of the culture on effectiveness – after all, this 90 per cent figure takes a bit of justifying! Suppose an individual goes to a seminar on personal time management and comes back to their organisation (church or otherwise) fired up to put some of the newly discovered principles into practice. If the culture of the organisation is characterised by statements like:

- 'We work better at the last minute under pressure.'
- 'Don't bother planning; you don't know what's going to happen.'
- 'It'll be all right on the night.'
- 'Planning denies the work of the Holy Spirit – we don't want that secular stuff round here!'

then it will be very difficult for the individual to implement the concepts that were shared at the seminar. The culture will overwhelm and dilute the ideas of the delegate. The worst thing they could say is, 'I learnt this on the course.' Usually they will be given a couple of tablets and the assumption is that they will be better in a few days! In a conflict between an individual's new ideas and their organisational culture, the prevailing culture will usually triumph.

We can summarise our key questions for this chapter as follows:

- How will the culture of the church support the discipler –learner relationship?
- What ingredients of the culture are enabling or inhibiting? To what extent?
- What credibility and influence does the coach/mentor have within the organisation?

Literature about the 'learning organisation' has been around for a number of years now without really having a significant impact on the writing, thinking and activity of churches. The better materials are just as applicable to discipling in churches as to development in other organisations. For a start, there are common threads that can be summarised in these core principles about learning:

1. Learning happens much of the time. If it is done deliberately and purposefully, rather than on an ad hoc basis, the quantity and quality will increase dramatically. Furthermore, there will be a better fit between learning and role or ministry.
2. It should be recognised that learning is continuous; there is no starting or finishing point. We should never cut budgets or change time priorities to limit learning, even for a short season. Integrated learning must stay near the top of our agenda.
3. The lessons of shared learning usually go deeper than those obtained through learning by ourselves, partly because the culture may become more conducive to their application.

The transmission and preservation of a learning culture is one of the prime leadership responsibilities, so it is critical that leaders model participation in the learning church, otherwise they become the change agents that worsen the culture. Remember that values are caught, not taught. Leaders must review successes and failures and seek to apply the lessons. They must ask questions, welcome feedback and not be seen to be above reproach. Leaders must be experimenting in their own lives, as well as with corporate activities. They must reinforce the learning culture by openly sharing about their own developmental experiences. Questions like 'What am I going to do better/differently?' should be as commonplace in their own thinking as in their expectations when others report to them.

In their attempts to develop other people, leaders need to score high in the desire to influence and they should have acquired a wide range of development skills. One of these features without the other will be insufficient. The combinations of the desire to influence and the skill level are summarised in the quadrants of the diagram or page 188. If their need to influence is far higher than their skill level, they will impose their solutions. In extreme cases, the dangers of domination and control will be very real. Probably the alternative is much less common: good skills but insufficient desire to influence. The facilitator quadrant sounds ideal, but the lack of impact will lessen the benefits of feedback and experience. The fourth quadrant (bottom left in diagram) does not match up with biblical leadership because the outcome is not developmental for other people; it's purely about learning along with the members. We discussed influencing in Chapter 12 and feedback in Chapter 9: they are two of the core skills of people development.

I have given some special attention to leaders because they model the corporate culture. If leaders don't model a

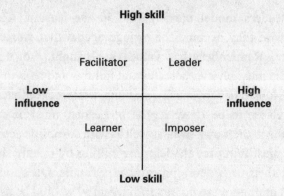

learning culture, the context will rapidly deteriorate for everybody else. Yet there should be many more indians than chiefs and we have already stressed that we are all called to disciple and be discipled. What attitudes can we expect to see in members who are involved in discipleship? I want us to consider the concepts of motivation and commitment. Motivated people have energy and drive and their fires are lit; we might describe them as 'switched-on' people. Committed people offer their contributions for the greater, corporate benefit. Again, we should be looking for both qualities. Motivation without commitment produces play, self-indulgence, selfishness and a butterfly-type flitting mentality. There's plenty of this about these days, focusing on the individual, their rights and self-fulfilment. Commitment without motivation produces drudgery, obligation and an overdeveloped sense of duty. We should be looking for a membership that is motivated and is prepared to sacrifice self for the common good.

In the table on page 190, I have illustrated some of the key contrasting ingredients that help and hinder learning. The pivotal issues include leadership style, communication style,

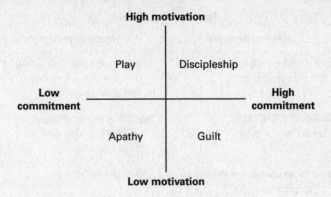

the attitude to new ideas, and how risk-taking and mistakes are treated.

Western culture nowadays is very competitive and generally assumes that an individual's success primarily occurs at the expense of other people. Maslow undertook some fieldwork among the Blackfoot Indian tribe and found that the whole climate sponsored and provoked development in a way that is quite alien to our present everyday experience (*Maslow on Management*, p. 24). He found the following:

1. An emphasis on generosity was the highest virtue of the tribe. Accumulating assets or knowledge received scant praise. Giving assets, knowledge and property away was what brought one true prestige and security within the tribe.

2. Extensive testing showed that members of this Indian tribe suffered less from self-doubt and self-consciousness than did people from more competitive environments and ways of life. It was as if each tribe member knew his or her strengths and weaknesses. Weaknesses were not ostracised but accepted as a normal part of the human condition.

The Learning Church

Helping features	*Hindering features*
Leader and member agree development plan.	Members are not committed to their own development. They feel powerless.
Discipleship is a major leadership priority.	Pressures of routine work preclude quality time for development.
Leadership style is involving and gives responsibility	Top-down autocracy.
An emphasis on teamwork.	Internal competition.
Long-term thinking.	Short-term thinking.
Admitting and owning inadequacies and errors.	Blaming other people or 'circumstances'.
Asking questions.	Silent submission and compliance.
Talking about learned lessons.	Talking about the event.
Being open about the real situation.	Filtering bad news or letting people hear what they want to hear.
Proposing and acting on new ideas.	Finding reasons why we can't implement them.
Use of different ways of learning.	A monochrome approach to learning, e.g. just focusing on reading or lecturing.
The bulk of the members take risks.	Most members are ultra-cautious.
Training is a major budget item.	Training is cut when funds are tight.
Training is reviewed and the lessons are integrated.	Training occurs in isolation to normal activity.

3. There was a strong emphasis on personal responsibility within the tribe, which began with the very young. Parents encouraged their children, from a very early age, to do things for themselves in the context of a very loving and supportive environment.

4. The needs of the tribe as a whole were effortlessly combined with the needs of the individual tribe members.

5. The tribe tended not to have general leaders with general powers, but rather they had different leaders for different functions. Each leader was chosen for a particular job, based on the needs of that job.

We should be challenged to ensure that the culture for the learning church is different from the culture of the bulk of the Western world. I would venture to suggest that if we cannot epitomise interdependence, as opposed to independence, then we are not radical enough and there will be little progress in our churches. Many qualities of the learning church are at odds with our prevailing national cultures.

We need to recognise the effect that a learning culture is bound to have on our church meetings. Progressively, the world is producing a consumer mentality that expects high standards. There is a danger of producing a sort of polished slickness. But there has to be room for people to learn, develop and acquire experience. As church members, we need to allow that space. I am not advocating that we offer the pulpit to all and sundry, but we should take risks with people who have shown some giftedness in that particular area of ministry. If all sermons were preached by the best preacher, who else would develop? If the best musicians, or even the most anointed worship leaders, were responsible for the music every week, where would be the growth? We need to remember the full heart behind Ephesians 4:11 – the purpose of those gifted functionaries is to equip the saints for the work of ministry. In the learning church, the music will be mediocre some mornings and some of the preaching might not be perfect theologically, yet, paradoxically, the flock will not suffer in the long term.

The challenge to leaders in this developmental culture is very real. Sometimes I wonder whether the real reluctance to release people is not that they might do damage, but that they might be too successful! The leaders of learning churches need to be very secure in themselves, and be at peace with their own vulnerabilities, weaknesses and temptations. It is easy to take responsibility for the bulk of the visible ministry; life is safe and predictable. As we develop other people, we often experience a roller-coaster existence. Your most promising disciples let you down or move away. Just as fruit seems to be imminent, you have to take the reins for a season again. At the same time, you have to struggle with your own learning and, as a learner, it's your responsibility to go where no one has gone before.

The contrast in this rather ill-defined existence can be painful, but people do not always see the results. I've been to churches as a consultant in the wake of some great speakers after they have moved on to other ministries. I am referring to speakers who could honestly say that people had regularly travelled many a mile to listen to their ministry. Yet after they had gone, the deposit in lives was sometimes pitifully small. There had been lots of inspirational teaching, but not much learning. There might have been a plaque on the wall, but real change in the lives of the members was limited. Polished 'perfection', driven by consumerism, is at odds with a culture of development; messy services are necessary, but only provided that we release the right people and they are committed to learning. A learning church does not describe a decade as one year of blunders repeated ten times over.

15

The Barriers to Discipling

The Great Commission is widely known, and faithful people are involved in discipling in all sorts of churches. I write this chapter, not because none is happening, but because more could be done if we thoroughly understood what hinders us. We need to look at the barriers to effective, sustained discipling. I hope that it will prove useful to highlight some of the key blockages I have seen across a wide spectrum of churches and to draw on the experiences of other people who have shared their insights with me. The headings that have given the shape to this chapter look remarkably similar to headings used in discussing why appraisal systems fail (see chapter 7 in *Leadership Tool Kit*). This shouldn't be surprising really, given that appraisals should be primarily driven by the desire to develop people.

Barriers in the discipler

There is often a presumption when something goes wrong that the 'junior' person is likely to be responsible. For example, in delegation, the delegator might be likely to see the attitude of the subordinate as a prime reason for the job not getting done, when this might not actually be the dominant reason. In a similar way, the discipler must take a full share of responsibility for the effectiveness of the discipling relationship. They should have the vision, skills and experience to carry the process through the more difficult seasons.

I believe that the basic issue is about volition. Do we really want to be making disciples? Most Christians would give a prompt affirmative response, but we need to look at what people *do*, not at what they *say*. Discipling is costly; we get hurt and frustrated, develop our own gifts less and, perhaps above all, it's very time demanding. I must be honest and say that leaders can fall into this trap as often as members, and often model too much *doing* and not enough *developing* of other people. The business world experiences the same difficulty: 'BP Chemicals carried out a series of surveys of graduates with up to two years' service and identified that many line managers were too engrossed in their other responsibilities to develop new staff as rapidly and as well as was required' (Hamilton, *Mentoring*, p. 25). We must become very different in the church. Too many leaders up to now have abdicated one of their major responsibilities: that of properly investing in other members. Discipling has not been the priority that should have driven their time management and diaries.

The second principal danger for disciplers is that they become too prescriptive and directive. If we are secure enough to realistically accept and value our own gifts from God, and (for us older ones) to acknowledge the wealth of experience we have accrued, then there is the danger of acting as though we have all the answers. Surely we can save the disciple many painful experiences if we solve their problems and dispense our wisdom? Perhaps the root of this attitude is also the desire to do discipleship quickly and to take a short cut to the best outcomes. In the cold light of day, we need to recognise that some lessons will only be learned by experience, and cannot be grasped from the recounted experiences of sages. Sometimes the easiest way to spot this danger is to look at what the discipler is trying to produce. If it's a replica of themselves, the process is likely to be flawed.

The third frequent blockage that is more the responsibility of the mentor lies in a confusion of roles. Many churches have a strong pyramid mentality; for example, intern, cell leader, zone supervisor, elder and itinerant. Some denominations might have fewer apparent strata, but membership of the Parochial Church Council or diaconate might carry substantial prestige. There can be difficulties of role in any organisation when we try to develop an immediate subordinate. It should be a requirement that we do try and develop the next 'tier', but there are limitations. Usually the easiest developmental role to fulfil is the coach, where the learning is based on the skills and knowledge that enable the disciple to do the job better. But partly because we also have a responsibility for achieving organisational goals alongside our subordinates, it is very much more difficult to mentor them. I have already said that being a manager and mentor to the same person is virtually impossible. In church life as well as 'normal' jobs, it may well be that the best mentors are external to our church or department. There are real benefits in a degree of distance and simplicity of role. I think that this is especially true for the mature believer.

The two final difficulties that I have observed in disciplers are less frequent and the solutions are easier to define. Many young Christians assume that they are too inexperienced to disciple others. There is a lack of confidence about what they have to offer. The answer involves a change of church culture, which is not simple and takes a few years. Eventually we have to foster the expectation that all members will disciple, and also be discipled. Just as it is good for all new members to take on one area of service, so an end product of any membership training course should be that people are involved in giving and receiving discipling. New converts are vulnerable and need protection, but they often make effective evangelists, for example. Their initial enthusiasm can enable them to provoke good practice in more cynical old-stagers.

Finally, a shortage of skills can limit our effectiveness as disciplers. However, I am much more interested in heart issues than I am worried about skill shortages as we turn our churches to a discipleship mentality. The key skill that is needed is that of questioning and I hope that you found Chapter 8 useful in this respect. My experience is that skill acquisition requires the learner to have moved at least from unconscious incompetence to conscious competence; that step seldom happens in the earliest stages.

Barriers in the disciple

A distorted self-image is one of the greatest barriers to personal growth. (Disciplers also need an accurate perspective on themselves!) Perhaps surprisingly, both an over-inflated opinion and an unrealistically poor assessment are harmful. In one sense, arrogance and self-debasement both deny the full work of the cross. A very high self-esteem may encourage an individual to deny that they need help. This sort of person may find difficulty in accepting and submitting to any type of authority as well. Nothing can be allowed to dint the façade of confidence! Even more disconcerting, some people don't see themselves in a consistent way; they flick-flack between a brittle confident image and a disparaging alternative. In these cases, the lower presentation is usually closer to how they really see themselves.

Possibly the main cluster of barriers in the disciple will be various forms of fear. Some may be well grounded, others may be quite irrational, but they will underpin the disciple's approach to development. Their construct of their reality is the foundation of their thinking. There are some people in our churches who have experienced a spiritual battering under the auspices of discipling. Some of the problems were partly of their own making, and include a failure to take personal responsibility, but that's not the full picture. I won't go so far as to use the word 'abuse' – in this 'PC' era, the word has lost the full meaning – nevertheless, certain styles of leadership have contributed to a fear of any form of discipling.

Fear is a complex and multi-dimensional subject that I do not feel competent to explore to any real depth. However, Lewis (*Mentoring Manager*, pp. 137–8) lists four particular areas of fear that deserve our attention, because he reckons that they occur frequently:

1. Fear of the unknown.
2. Fear of scrutiny.
3. Fear of failure.
4. Fear of the relationship.

Breaking new ground is always a challenge, but individuals vary dramatically in their desire to experience the unknown. For some people, challenge is meat and drink; for others uncertainty cripples them. We need to know disciples very well, and not assume their comfort zones are similar in size to ours, big or small.

For those who fear scrutiny, at least the prescription is easy to describe. If we handle the first signs of their faults positively and magnanimously, we will encourage disciples to open up further. For many folk it is a considerable shock to be known well and yet still to be accepted and loved. I think that establishing a mentality of perpetual learning best solves the fear of failure. If hurdles are rare, the memories of pass or fail will remain very strong between the tests. But if every day has learning opportunities, we can raise the bar gradually.

The final fear could be considered as a concern that the relationship might become too intimate. People who have been repeatedly bruised in relationships may be cautious about getting too close to other people, in case they get hurt again. However, there are also those who seek out hurtful relationships and will engineer abuse. As disciplers, we must not push for too much relationship too quickly; neither should we offer more than we can sustain.

My final barrier in the disciple is that the good can become the enemy of the best. Over a period of time, we hope to see their expectations raised from the qualities in the central column of the table on page 200 to the heights of the right-hand features.

Barriers in the relationship

With the best will in the world from both parties, the spark between the discipler and disciple sometimes just doesn't happen. The problem can partly emanate from the structures of the discipling process: beyond the spontaneous combinations, how is it decided who works with whom? We've referred

The bad	The good	The best
Selfishness	Altruism	Servanthood
Dependence	Able to stand on their own feet	Interdependence
Over-negative/ positive self-image	Accurate self-image	Security 'in Christ Jesus'
Need for certainty	Comfortable with ambiguity	Proactive in personal changes
Ignorance	Understanding	Wisdom and insight
Low levels of ability	High levels of ability	A consistent learning mentality

to this difficulty in Chapter 5. When a particular combination is deemed by both parties to be a long way from ideal, it's probably best to break up the partnership and put them in other pairs. I've usually found that such difficulties are not just a personality clash, which is a very general description, but more frequently the differences are rooted in values. I've never yet met a church discipling structure that has the resources to get to the bottom of the bulk of these differences, nor do I suspect that the chemistry of interpersonal relationships can always be made to work; there is no such universal catalyst.

Sometimes the problems are easier to solve, especially if they are spotted at an early stage. People can embark on a developmental relationship with very different expectations of the process. I got this badly wrong in mentoring the managers of a well-known UK mission. We didn't allow enough time to sell the process and, while accepting and knowing that the outcomes would be different for the different managers, the boundaries and limits were not defined sufficiently. I believe that two managers made considerable progress over the course of a couple of years, many other managers were satisfied with the outcome, but two people gained very little ground. That was a steep learning curve for me. I could have served them better with a clearly defined process and better exploration of the boundaries and expectations. In any discipling process, the earliest meetings set a tenor which is not easily changed.

Another common problem where all parties can take responsibility is connected with the pace of learning. Sometimes expectations are ridiculously high, fostering an unhealthy intensity. The counter-danger is stressing the relationship to the detriment of development – then the meetings can become just social events. The final common danger is a lack of confidentiality, leading to a loss of trust.

Barriers in the systems and culture

Given the overriding importance of the corporate culture, the single biggest barrier to discipling is an unsupportive culture, exhibiting the *opposite* elements to those we described in the last chapter. Culture is modelled and transmitted by leaders, so their overt support and involvement is simply critical to discipling being commonplace. Their commitment to the process needs to be evident in their own discipling and the importance that the developing of other people has in their diaries. I have seen many churches, both with cell mentality and other types of structure, try to disciple via the small group meeting. This works well, but only to a certain ceiling. The needs of the group are normally too widespread to be met jointly and simultaneously. Another difficulty is that the sequence of the four 'Ws' in the group meeting is usually welcome, worship, word and finally works/witness. Inevitably the last ingredient is often squeezed for time. I do recognise wholeheartedly, however, that administratively discipling can occur via the cell community, not primarily the cell meeting. There is a real danger of producing a church discipling package that is too dependent on printed materials rather than skilled teachers. As we have already said, the key skill is the ability to ask the right questions within a climate of trust. While this skill is developed and acquired, members naturally want some framework to their discipling meetings. Too often the end product is over-reliance on a manual of some sort. I've seen churches get locked into a scheme that isn't working, unable to find a way out. Discipling meetings can then end up slavishly and woodenly plodding through the prescribed chapter. The root of the danger of course is that central leadership has presumed that the same material will be pertinent for everybody.

Barriers to learning

I'm finding the whole subject of adult learning quite fascinating. At times it can be rather painful as I reflect on my failures to maximise learning opportunities and on my efforts to help other people. There is a range of conceptual blocks that can hamper development. These include:

1. The assumption that a problem has a more narrow focus than it actually has.
2. Failure to investigate the apparently obvious.
3. Failure to distinguish between cause and effect.
4. Failure to consider the problem from the perspectives of different people.

I have fallen into all of these traps as I have attempted to help people manage their family finances. Here are the respective examples, taken from four different situations:

1. Wilfully overspending, believing that an imminent legacy would solve everything.
2. The Inland Revenue had mistakenly left them on their (emergency) tax code.
3. The fact that the bailiffs hadn't come encouraged them to think things were OK.
4. The husband and wife saw totally different reasons for why they were in debt.

When I watch quiz programmes, I am often surprised at the lack of biblical knowledge in the general public. Some of these people are now joining churches! We can make vast false assumptions about people's theological background and vocabulary. Perhaps the language problem is deeper than just the use of a technical term; for example, I wonder what percentage of our congregations could accurately describe the difference between justification and sanctification? Clear teaching of sound doctrine is vital. I saw a similar, linguistic problem some years ago when, as a secondary school teacher, I was head of the mathematics department. We were having difficulty selecting materials for the eleven-year-old pupils. When I consulted teachers in the English department about some of my possible textbooks, it transpired that most of the maths textbooks for that age group required a reading age of twelve. Many kids that we thought were having problems with their maths could never wade through the prose to understand the question! I strongly suspect that some church jargon presents a similar difficulty, especially in a multi-cultural society.

Action plan

Set aside one of your discipling meetings to identify the biggest barriers to good fruit. Assume that there are some blockages in each of the discipler, the disciple, the culture and the approach to learning.

16

How We See People

In order that we can disciple people, we need to see potential disciples with wise eyes. A pair of massive bifocals will do, where one lens enables us to see people as they are now, and the other has a clear vision of who and what they can become in the future. As far as is humanly possible, this means looking at them as God does. God is love, he defines love, he is the epitome of love, and his character and nature are love. In the rough and tumble of discipling, we will need buckets of sacrificial love to sustain us all in the challenges to our relationships.

We frequently read in the gospels that Jesus was moved by or filled with compassion (e.g. Matthew 9:36; 14:14; 15:32; 20:34). The same qualities are a prerequisite in discipleship. Rejoicing when they rejoice, hurting when they hurt, mourning when they mourn, empathy is a prime biblical basis for sharing lives. While I believe that in some churches we have overemphasised the role of the pastoral ministry to the detriment of apostles, prophets and evangelists, nevertheless something of the heart of a pastor is the first condition for effective discipling.

In the creation account of Genesis, we are told that we have been created in the image of God. That speaks of unlimited potential in redeemed humankind with and under the power of the Holy Spirit. I cannot think of any biblical limitations placed on the optimum possible fulfilment of our potential. It's vital that we see the disciples whom we serve in exactly this same way as we draw closer to God in character. They have massive potential, and to see that released we are called to make tremendous sacrifices.

As always, the outworking and expression of our sacrificial love is wide open to a range of applications and interpretation, so long as we seek God's will and stay within the confines of Scripture. We will be called to love in a variety of ways. I want to suggest some very practical flesh on the bones, some principles that should undergird our approach. When we are available as coaches or mentors, it's important that our attitudes in discipleship are right, as well as our actions. Here are some key assumptions about how we need to view people.

Assume that generally people are trustworthy

I am not making a completely blind statement here; there are very definitely some people who have consistently proved that they cannot be trusted in certain ways – it's the only consistent thing about them! It would be rash and foolish to give them responsibility beyond a certain level. But I am referring here to the vast majority of people and the principle of reaping and sowing. We have already said in Chapter 6 that trust involves risk but assumes a positive response from people generally. Sometimes we should make the risk element clear to people as we stretch the existing boundaries: 'I'd like you to have a go at this. I appreciate that this responsibility is more than you've experienced before, but we've been delighted with all your recent progress. It's a fresh level of opportunity.' My contention is that the usual response will be positive; people will rise to such trust. Certainly, it is the coach/mentor's job to take risks of trust, knowing that people will let us down from time to time. We also have to illustrate how to cope with such disappointments. The alternative stifles development.

Assume that people have a substantial capacity to grow

The psychologist Abraham Maslow coined the phrase 'self-actualisation', which I have only encountered in the context of his triangular diagram, representing the hierarchy of human needs. Self-actualisation is his title for the highest of the five levels of human need (above survival, security, belonging and contributing). Broadly speaking, it refers to an in-built mechanism for personal development. He believes, and so do I, that we all have a capacity to enhance our skills, knowledge and circumstances. In the wrong organisational climate, which unfortunately does not exclude every church, such an expectation of growth can become quite dulled.

Understand that communication is vital to providing a secure climate for growth

Everyone should be kept informed as much as possible of things relevant to their situation. We should scrutinise reasons for withholding information and work on the basis that leaders should tell people as much as they can and as soon as they can. Wide, deliberate communication is one of the single most important factors in establishing and sustaining a climate of trust. There will be many ambiguities to live with in the discipling process without us adding to these tensions unnecessarily.

Stress the benefits of corporate life

The focus of this book has been on personal and individual development, while commenting on the corporate benefits. But the New Testament talks repeatedly about our shared existence in the body of Christ. One of the themes of this book has been the importance of interdependence, and that this lifestyle is a vastly richer experience than autonomy or independence. Team-working, togetherness, a sense of corporate identity, an esprit de corps, and a sense of belonging all contribute to learning. Any development that can be done together will be deemed by most of the population to be more fun. Just finding out that other people are 'in the same (or similar) boat' is a great encouragement.

Work on the basis that inappropriate reaction will be followed by measured response

The initial riposte to feedback or suggestions that we might like to consider certain changes is often negative and defensive. If we state these reactions in graphic, volatile language, it is difficult to rescind when the dust has settled. Both parties have a major responsibility to make their joint life easier when changes are first mooted. The coach/mentor should not require complete compliance immediately or assume that there is a grave character weakness if the initial reaction is less than all-embracing. The disciple should consider the suggestions and delay responding rather than react immediately; it's hard to backtrack from a blanket dismissal of a proposal.

Usually poor (immediate) reactions are not a true and accurate comment on the person's attitude. Wait for their measured responses before assessing their desire and capability to change.

Treat people as individuals

Time constraints encourage us all to disciple people in groups whenever possible. Probably, therefore, we do not spend enough time thinking about, praying about and exploring individual differences. Another compounding factor is the dangerous assumption that the best outcome of discipling looks remarkably like us! People have a strong desire to be seen as unique rather than anonymous or interchangeable. Whenever we acknowledge a person's individuality, their response is likely to scale new heights.

Respect people's decisions

I hope you will agree with me when I say that this statement has been one of the core themes of this book. People are far more likely to do what they say than what we tell them to do. Sometimes they will come to conclusions and priorities for change that, in our wisdom, we would not have prescribed. Don't worry; there's more than one way to skin a cat. Usually the order of change is not critical, and if folk will move forward in any positive way, that's better than prevaricating about the first steps of our recommended syllabus. It is also simply arrogance for us to assume that we know the best decisions for their lives. Sometimes people will fall flat on their faces when they act on their own conclusions. That's part of the learning process, and for the life of me I'm not sure that we can always prevent it from happening. Neither is it wise to try to save them from this apparent calamity.

Assume that people are courageous enough to sustain the discipling process

There is a danger, based on a genuine concern to minimise risk and possible hurt, that we set and transmit expectations that are below the disciple's real capacity for progress. I believe that there are many folk in our churches who are inwardly screaming for discipling. Possibly they don't understand the future cost, but again it's not rightfully our decision to protect them from such issues. We must work on the basis that people can take it, that they are tough, strong and durable. I am primarily talking about spiritual and emotional stamina, not physical. We can always adjust our assessments and advice, but I would much rather err on the optimistic side than over-protection. It's about showing our faith in them and confidence in the Holy Spirit.

Remember that most people in the church have the same basic and central objectives

A leader who is passionate about a vision for the future of the church may be tempted to focus too quickly on the detail. When we look at the small print, people are bound to give different weight to different aspects of the vision; it's natural, considering that they will have a range of complementary gifts. The danger is that we start to focus on difference rather than stressing the common ground. Church members are volunteers and they don't give up their time and money lightly, at least not on a sustained basis. Work on the basis that most people share the same big picture as you. I've always encouraged folk to persevere through difficult times if the area of disagreement is a goal or priority. If the problem is vision or values, the problem probably won't go away. Eventually somebody will leave. Initially, it is best to assume that those who show serious commitment share the same hopes.

Years ago, I studied the management of change applied to the education sector. The transition from a tripartite structure (grammar, technical and secondary modern) to comprehensive schooling was virtually complete. One of the arguments that had been put forward in favour of comprehensive schools was that the old system produced self-fulfilling prophecies. If, based on the results of the eleven-plus examination, you told children that they were good, then they usually did well. Sending them to a secondary modern school was a message that you expected them to do badly, and behold that was often the outcome. Church members are very similar. You will transmit your expectations of them to them over a period of time. Your optimism or otherwise will be communicated by all sorts of messages. If we are going to make a contribution to discipling, our view of the potential disciple, and how we communicate that view, is critical.

Conclusion

In the Introduction, I mentioned my prime reason for writing this book. The twin impossible peaks of church life used to be evangelism and discipleship. Whilst real progress has been made on the practicalities of undertaking evangelism, my observation is that we need to see a major breakthrough in discipleship. I believe that God has ordained Alpha and the whole thrust of personal evangelism; this book is driven by a passion that God wants us to return to biblically based discipleship as well. When I first started to gather material for this book, I looked at what Scripture has to show us about some of the discipling relationships; for example Moses and Joshua, Elijah and Elisha, Paul and Timothy. We have very little detail about how the disciple developed. All we know is that they spent many years together, focusing on doing what God asked of them.

There are some major causes of pessimism in my desire to see widespread discipling, including many models of ministry, the style of training for leadership and the culture of most churches right across the denominations. These negative concerns are far outweighed by the key observations recorded in this book. First, when in doubt, I return to the Great Commission and continue to conclude that God wants everybody to be discipled and to be discipling. Since the process is not limited to the work of leaders, the insights cannot be in the league of rocket science and must be accessible to us all. The subset of discipling that I have called mentoring involves listening, asking questions and offering a sense of perspective. Spiced with lashings of encouragement, this level of discipling seems to be within the grasp of all of us, although we will reach different standards of proficiency in our ability to ask the right questions.

To illustrate, a worthwhile discipling session can revolve around these questions:

- In what three major areas have you grown in the last twelve months?
- In what major areas do you feel called to develop in the next year?
- Apart from God, whose help will you require?
- What will be the first step in each area?
- How will these steps help you fulfil your vision?
- What could be the most serious obstacles?

A cynic might say that if the above questions cover the first meeting, what happens afterwards? The style of some of the questions will permit many repetitions and the answers to other questions are a lifetime of exploration.

More excitement comes from the promise in 1 Corinthians 12:7, where we are told, 'To each one the manifestation of the Spirit is given for the common good.' Many church members feel overwhelmed at the idea that they have gifts and that part of the expression of that giftedness is to develop other people in similar ministries. Essentially, everybody can coach in something! Remember that the basis of coaching is modelling, not teaching.

Another area for optimism was mentioned in Chapter 2: the principle laid down in 2 Timothy 2:2. Our challenge as leaders is not just to produce disciples but disciple-makers. The verse talks about four generations being involved. Let's look at a mathematical model. If one person could contribute to the discipling of five people, and teach each of those people the same principles, then there would be twenty-five people in the third generation and 125 in the fourth. My belief is that we only need a relatively small number of people to start the discipling ball rolling, and that if it is done properly, discipleship can quickly become commonplace.

I suspect that the greatest barrier to discipling for many people is the question of the legitimacy of influencing other people. The concept smacks of manipulation and control. My defence, again, is in Scripture; we are told to 'make disciples', which sounds to be a conscious, legitimate and deliberate lifestyle. Certainly, we will need to check our motives and approach regularly, but avoidance, for fear of the dangers, is not a recommended option.

I am conscious that I have been harsh, not only on formal programmes for discipling, but also on the effectiveness of most teaching ministries, including sermons. This stance has been a little unfair. Actually, I am not against the traditional presentation of the word, but in isolation, without additional discipling, the fruit seems to be limited. We are clearly instructed: 'Let the word of Christ dwell in you richly as you teach and admonish one another with all wisdom, and as you sing psalms, hymns and spiritual songs with gratitude in your hearts to God' (Colossians 3:16). Disciplers and disciples should steep themselves in the word – perhaps this is the principal stepping-stone to a culture of widespread discipling. This is where the character and promises of God are revealed.

Bibliography

Anderson and Reese, *Spiritual Mentoring*, Guildford, Surrey: Eagle, 1999.

Arnold, J. Heinrich, *Discipleship*, Robertsbridge, E. Sussex: Plough Publishing House, 1994.

Belbin, R. Meredith, *Management Teams, Why They Succeed or Fail*, Oxford: Heinemann Professional Publishing, 1981.

Blanchard, K. and Peale, Norman Vincent, *The Power of Ethical Management*, New York: Morrow, 1988.

Boak, George, *Developing Managerial Competencies*, London: Pitman, 1991.

Brinkerhoff and Gill, *The Learning Alliance*, San Francisco: Jossey-Bass, 1994.

Buckland, Colin, *Liberated to Lead*, Eastbourne: Kingsway, 2001.

Cialdini, Robert B., *Influence*, Illinois: Foreman and Company, 1988.

Collins, Gary R., *Christian Coaching*, Colorado: NavPress, 2001.

Dixon, Nancy M., *The Organizational Learning Cycle*, Aldershot, Hants: Gower, 1999.

Eales-White, Rupert, *The Power of Persuasion*, London: Kogan Page, 1992.

England, Edward (ed.), *Keeping a Spiritual Journal*, Godalming: Highland Books, 1988.

Fitzgerald and Kirby, *Developing Leaders, Research and Applications in Psychological Type and Leadership Development*, Palo-Alto, California: Davies-Black Publishing, 1997.

Fritts, Patricia, *The New Managerial Mentor*, Palo-Alto, California: Davies-Black Publishing, 1998.

Garret, Bob, *Creating a Learning Organisation*, Cambridge: Director Books, 1990.

Garret, Bob, *The Learning Organization*, London: HarperCollins, 1994.

Garvin, David A., *Learning in Action*, Boston, Massachusetts: Harvard Business School Press, 2000.

Goleman, Daniel, *Emotional Intelligence*, London: Bloomsbury Books, 1996.

Greenman, William D., *Purpose, Destiny and Achievement*, USA: Destiny Image, 1998.

Hall, Douglas T. and Associates, *Career Development in Organisations*, San Francisco and London: Jossey-Bass, 1988.

Hamilton, Reg, *Mentoring*, London: The Industrial Society, 1993.

Hargreaves, Jennifer, *Sporting Females*, London: Routledge, 1994.

Haslam, Greg, *Elisha: a Sign and a Wonder*, Eastbourne: Kingsway Publications, 1995.

Herriot, Peter, *The Career Management Challenge*, London: Sage, 1992.

Higgs, Malcolm and Dulewicz, Victor, *Making Sense of*

Emotional Intelligence, USA: ASE, NFER-Nelson, 1999.

Houston, James M., *The Mentored Life*, Colorado: NavPress, 2002.

Isaacs, William, *Dialogue and the Art of Thinking Together*, New York: Doubleday, 1999.

Klug, Ron, *How to Keep a Spiritual Journal*, Minneapolis: Augsburg, 2002.

Kotter, John P., *Power and Influence*, New York: Free Press, 1985.

LeFever, Marlene, *Learning Styles*, Eastbourne: Kingsway Publications, 1998.

Lewis, Gareth, *Mentoring Manager*, Great Britain: Prentice Hall, 1996.

Lucas, Jeff, *Elijah: Anointed and Stressed*, Eastbourne: Kingsway Publications, 1995.

MacLennan, Nigel, *Coaching and Mentoring*, Aldershot, Hants: Gower, 1988.

Mallison, John, *Mentoring to Develop Disciples and Leaders*, Adelaide: Scripture Union and Openbook Publishers, 1998.

Maxwell, John C., *Developing the Leader Within You*, Nashville: Nelson, 1993.

Maxwell, John C., *Developing the Leaders Around You*, Nashville: Nelson, 1995.

Megginson and Boydell, *A Manager's Guide to Coaching*, London: BACIE, 1979.

Mowry, Bill, *What If You Taught and No One Learned?*, Colorado Springs: The Navigators, 1995.

Ortiz, Juan Carlos, *Disciple: A Handbook for New Believers*, Lake Mary, Florida: Creation House, 1975

New, George and Cormack, David, *Why Did I Do That?*, London: Hodder & Stoughton, 1997.

Parsloe, Eric, *Coaching, Mentoring and Assessing*, London: Kogan Page, 1992.

Parsloe, Eric, *The Manager as Coach and Mentor*, London: IPD, 1995.

Pentecost, J. Dwight, *Design for Discipleship*, Grand Rapids, Michigan: Zondervan, 1971.

Peterson and Hicks, *Leader as Coach*, Minneapolis: Personal Decisions International, 1996.

Pfeffer, Jeffrey, *Power in Organizations,* London: Pitman, 1981.

Reynolds, Larry, *The Trust Effect*, London: Nicholas Brealey Publishers, 1997.

Rose, Colin, *Accelerated Learning*, Aylesbury, Bucks: Accelerated Learning Systems Ltd, 1985.

Smith and Dodds, *Developing Managers Through Project-Based Learning*, Aldershot, Hants: Gower, 1997.

Stanley and Clinton, *Connecting*, Colorado Springs: NavPress, 1992.

Thom, Cleland, *Moses: the Making of a Leader*, Eastbourne: Kingsway Publications, 1996.

Walker, T.W., *Aim for Excellence*, Basingstoke: Marshall-Pickering, 1988.

Watkinson, Duncan, *An Introduction to Discipleship*, Goa, India: New Frontiers International, 1995.

Wilkinson, Dr Bruce, *The Seven Laws of the Learner*, Oregon: Multnomah Press, 1992.

Leadership Tool Kit

by Bryn Hughes

After nearly twenty years in management training, Bryn Hughes is convinced that enhancing the skills of leadership is critical for ministers of churches, leaders of missions and other Christian organisations. These skills come into sharp focus when training the crucial second tier of leadership.

However, leaders who are committed to improving both themselves and their senior teams are desperately short of practical tools. Here is a development manual of eleven tested tools, including:

- exploring motives
- identifying key result areas
- learning from success – and failure
- delegation and communication
- continuing self-development

Liberated to Lead

by Colin Buckland

This unique book is designed to enhance the effectiveness of full-time leaders in Christian ministry or mission. Used prayerfully, the exercises and points for reflection will enable you to:

- balance family life and the pressures of ministry
- cultivate a healthy attitude to power in ministry roles
- settle on realistic expectations in ministry
- gain an introduction to self-awareness skills
- clarify your sense of calling to Christian service
- avoid unnecessary sexual problems
- overcome or prevent burnout

THE REVD COLIN D BUCKLAND has more than 23 years' experience as a pastor, and more than 18 years' as a consultant, trainer and counsellor to church leaders, churches and Christian organisations.

FUTURECHURCH